# 50 CRAFT IDEAS with PATTERNS

by Loretta E. Reese

illustrated by Lorraine Arthur

STANDARD PUBLISHING
Cincinnati, Ohio          2144

Library of Congress Catalog Card Number: 80-53363

ISBN: 0-87239-427-1

# PREFACE

The engine and caboose in my first book (*54 Crafts With Easy Patterns*—2134) were so popular, I have designed a complete train storage set of eight pieces. It is designed so that you may couple all the cars together with Velcro fastener material. All eight pieces are nearly the same size.

Corrugated cardboard is my favorite material, as you may have guessed from the many times it appears in my crafts. It is readily available, and so easily cut with an electric saber saw. (If you have never used a saber saw, try it! They are not expensive. When using it, however, do keep your fingers away from the blade. It's not the type of tool to use while watching television, or when you have any other distraction.)

I'm very grateful to God for giving me Christian parents, an understanding Christian husband, and a logical mind. All these were combined to bring about this book and enable me to share God's gift with you.

Most of these crafts were designed and used in my home congregation. Some are completely new designs. We used the train set in our vacation Bible school.

I especially appreciate my husband for being so patient and understanding. Our home certainly does get messy with crafts at times. But it's for the glory of God and gives His Biblical lessons lasting meaning for children.

*Loretta E. Reese*

# CONTENTS

# MATERIALS AND HOW TO USE THEM

## Hinges

Since writing *54 Crafts With Easy Patterns*, I have discovered another hinge material (interfacing) that works better than sheer nylon. It is superior since it is easily covered, doesn't fray, is very strong, has no trapped air bubbles or rippling in the drying process, cuts easily with scissors, and is very lightweight. It resembles fiberglass in appearance and is white. Hinges from this should be 1¼" to 1½" wide and about 1½" to 1¾" long. Doubled and glued to the underside of a hinged lid, they make ideal pull tabs.

## Eyes

Moving eyes are becoming more and more expensive. With two sizes of paper punches, you can make your own eyes of black and white construction paper. By using an oval punch, you can make different shaped eyes. Punch out lots of smaller circles of black paper. With a toothpick, put very tiny dots of white glue on white, blue, green, brown, red, or yellow paper. With a dampened finger, transfer a black dot to the background paper dotted with glue. Press down lightly. Turn a larger punch upside down, so you can peer through the hole and see the black dot. The black dot can be centered, or punched so it is on the edge of the punch hole. Experiment with them. I make lots of them at one time and put them in capped plastic pill bottles. If the bottle is amber, I glue an eye to the lid. With a tiny dot of glue, children can easily use them on projects.

## Gift Wrap

Don't overlook packages of gift wrap at your dime stores, etc. I always check displays for designs to use on projects. Purchase two packages of a kind, as they change designs periodically. Look for tiny birds and flowers, etc. If the child is very young, I'd suggest you glue the gift wrap designs to another paper with rubber cement to make it easier to glue to a project.

## Storage Projects

Almost any project made for storage can be converted to a bank by not using hinges or pull tabs. Just glue the lids shut, and then cut a slot. Any bank can be converted to a storage box by making one

piece with a hinge. Then either glue a pull tab, or overlap one of the pieces to open it.

## Rubber Cement

This is a great bonding cement when used to give a thin paper extra body. It makes designs easier for children to glue. It is very helpful in making durable designs for room decorations. In attaching a design to a window, mirror, or a block wall, cement the back of the design. If the design is large, use several dots of cement. Lightly press the design to the wall and remove. Now you can see where the dots are on both the wall and design. Recoat both the design and wall cement spots and allow to dry. Align the dots of cement and press firmly. (If you want the design to show on the outside of a window, coat the spots to receive cement with clear fingernail polish. When dry, coat the spots with rubber cement and follow the procedure just given.)

To remove, carefully pry the design up from behind with your fingers, pulling gently away. Turn it over and rub the rubber cement off the design and wall or window. Store the design for future use.

## Circle Tracings

Save a large number of metal or rigid plastic bottle lids so they nest inside one another. They will require little storage area, and you'll have just the right size to trace a circle. They are easier to use than coins. Make tracings on light cardboard by tracing around various sized bowls, saucers, lids, jars, plates, etc. Store these in a large mailing envelope for a real time-saver.

## Acetone

Acetone is the base for fingernail polish remover. Put some on a paper towel to rub off printing from margarine tubs, lids, and bottles. It will dissolve Styrofoam-type plastics (egg cartons). However, if you don't rub with pressure or put too much acetone on the towel, it is possible to take printing off such material. Experiment with it.

## Flatten Wallpaper

Unmanageable rolls of wallpaper used in covering various projects will flatten out quite nicely if you set your iron on the cotton setting and iron the back of them. Store the pieces, designed side down, on a flat surface until ready to use.

## Painting Macaroni Beads

String the beads on a chenille wire or a plastic straw that has been slit lengthwise with sharp scissors. Paint them and stick them in a pierced egg carton, Styrofoam cup, or corrugated box. Acrylic and airplane enamel paints dry in a reasonable period.

## Corrugated Cardboard Edges

There are two ways to give corrugated cardboard edges a more finished look. Glue narrow strips of construction paper or wallpaper to them. Run white glue over holes and channeled edges to close them. Paint will go over dried white glue very nicely.

## Electric Saber Saw With Knife-Edge Blade

This is a much used tool when working with corrugated cardboard. It is very reasonable in price. The knife-edge blade has no teeth. A mill file about six inches long is needed to keep the blade sharp. Blades dull rapidly if you cut much corrugated cardboard.

Many projects require the grain to run a certain way for added strength or a better gluing edge. Stack either two or four pieces of equal size together. Secure them on all four sides with pieces of masking tape. This keeps shifting down to a bare minimum during the sawing. Trace patterns on the top cardboard. The cardboard stacking should be with every other piece having the printed side up (if printing is on them). This will help you to keep the printed sides toward the inside of your projects. Paint does not readily cover printing on boxes.

To prevent breaking, blades should be allowed to cool when they are hot. Work slowly. Do not force the saber saw forward with pressure. Be very careful to stay exactly on the traced lines. Cuts will be very smooth. Remember, unplug the saw when you are sharpening the blade with light pressure on your file. Sharpen your blade from the back to the front of the blade. Put a piece of plywood on the table to cut cardboard.

## Glue

Children tend to put too much glue on projects. Encourage them to put a little glue in a plastic lid or cut down plastic creamer cup. Use the glue by applying it with a finger.

## Glue Bottles

Glue bottles, which have become unusable, can be dismantled with a tableware knife and pressure under the colored top cap. Nut cracking pliers work well on stuck caps. When the two parts of the cap are separated, clean them thoroughly. A fingernail file or small hooked crochet hook will enable you to loosen hardened glue in difficult to reach places. Before assembling, coat the grooved screw surfaces with a light coating of vegetable shortening. Screw the cap on, and with pressure push the top cap down and screw to tighten. Don't allow anyone to poke the clogged holes with scissors.

# HELPFUL HINTS

## Tracing and Transferring a Pattern

To transfer a pattern from this book to the paper you are going to use, tape a piece of tracing paper or thin typing paper over the pattern. Trace with a soft-lead pencil. Turn tracing over onto paper to be used and retrace design on back of typing or tracing paper with a hard-lead pencil. By doing it this way, your work will be neater, since no pencil marks will show on the right side.

If you are going to make several of the same item, tape the paper with the traced design on cardboard and cut out. This pattern can be used again and again by drawing around it.

Another way to transfer patterns would be to blacken the back of a traced design with a soft-lead pencil, if you wish to transfer to a light-colored paper. Tape tracing, back side down, to paper you wish to use. Go over the lines of traced design on the right side with a hard-lead pencil. For dark-colored paper use chalk instead of a pencil on the back of tracing paper.

## Scoring at Folds

To make cardboard or paper fold easily, run the blade of a pair of scissors or a dull knife lightly along fold line. Hold ruler against line as a guide to assure a straight fold.

## Enlarging or Reducing a Pattern

Trace the pattern. Mark off this tracing with half-inch squares. Next, square off a piece of paper the size you wish the pattern to be. If you want to make the pattern larger, make the squares larger. If you want to make the pattern smaller, make the squares smaller. Number the squares the same way on both sheets. Place sheets next to each other and reproduce design on second sheet, one square at a time. Check numbers for correct position.

## Curling Paper

To curl ends of paper, wrap the paper around a pencil and pull tight, or hold part of strip of paper between closed blade of scissors and thumb. Pull scissors gently but firmly along strip to end.

## Cutting and Gluing

Use a large pair of scissors or X-acto knife to cut cardboard and large areas if you do not have a saber saw. Use a small pointed pair of scissors to cut little things. Rubber cement is best for gluing large areas. White glue is fine for all other parts.

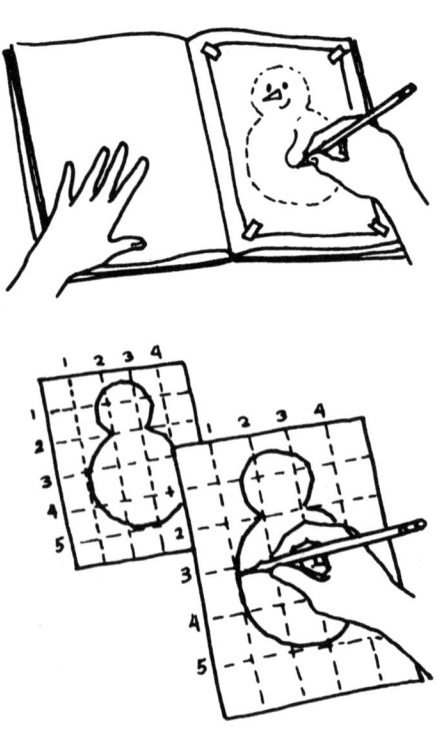

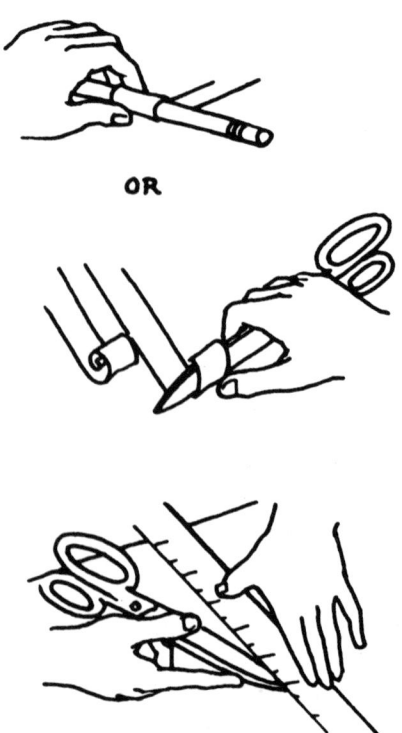

OR

# GENERAL CRAFTS

## Mailbox Verse Holder

*Materials needed:*
    Corrugated cardboard
    Light cardboard 3½" x 6" and ½" x 6⅛"
    ⅜" paper fastener
    Silver, gray, or whatever you choose paper to
        cover box
    Red construction paper
    White construction paper (optional)
    White glue
    Ice pick
    ⅛" paper punch
    Very thin interfacing (1½" x 1½") for hinge
    Electric saber saw with knife-edge blade

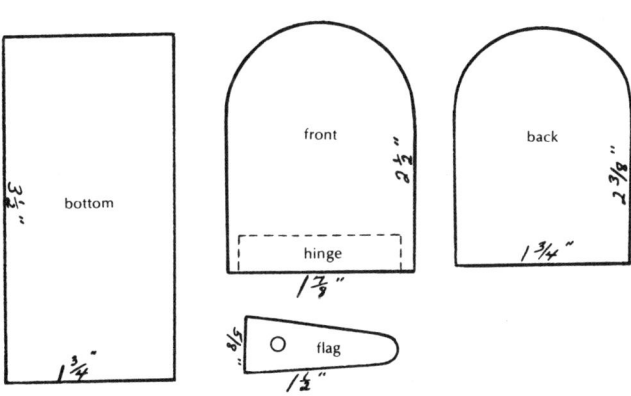

*Assembly:*
    With the saber saw and knife-edge blade, cut out all corrugated parts. Cut the light cardboard pieces out. Glue red construction paper to light cardboard for the flag. Punch a hole with the paper punch in the flag as indicated. Glue a piece of interfacing 1½" x 1½" to the corrugated bottom, then to the bottom of the corrugated door piece and up the front of the door piece. Allow to dry. You can print your name and house number on small pieces of white construction paper to be glued onto the front and side of the completed box.

Glue the back piece of corrugated material to the bottom of the mailbox, keeping close to the edge of the bottom piece. Glue the light cardboard strip to the front mailbox door. It will overlap the side of the mailbox on all sides except the bottom. It helps to bend light cardboard around your fingers to form a curve. Glue the sidepiece to the bottom and end of the mailbox.

Cut covering construction paper or paper of your choice. Glue the coverings over all cardboard surfaces. Glue the name to the side and house number to the front of the mailbox. Above the name, and back from the closed door, punch a hole from the outside of the mailbox toward the inside. Put a paper fastener through the red flag and box hole. Open it on the inside of the mailbox.

Type memory verses and put them inside the box. The flag can be used to indicate all memory verses are learned or they are not yet committed to memory.

## Radio Bank

*Materials needed:*
    Corrugated cardboard
    Light cardboard 2" x 9½" with center slot
        1½" x ³/₁₆"
    Woodtone wallpaper
    Black marking pen
    White glue
    Single edge razor blade
    Fingernail scissors
    Paper punch
    Electric saber saw with knife-edge blade
    Material such as colorful burlap 4" x 3½"

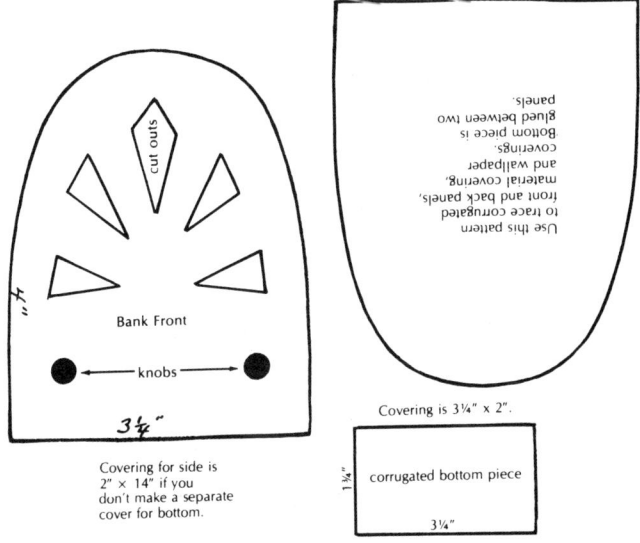

Use this pattern to trace corrugated front and back panels, material covering, and wallpaper coverings. Bottom piece is glued between two panels.

Covering is 3¼" x 2".

corrugated bottom piece
3¼"

Covering for side is 2" x 14" if you don't make a separate cover for bottom.

Bank Front
cut outs
knobs
3½"

The Word of God is beamed from our radio, if we but search for the Christian radio stations. You will need to explain this bank is like the radios of long ago. It is also a good class bank if your children are giving offerings to support a Christian radio station or program.

Cut all parts from materials indicated. Glue the cloth material to a corrugated domed piece. Cut the inner cutouts from the domed light cardboard with fingernail scissors. Glue this piece to woodtone wallpaper. Following the cutouts already done, cut the wallpaper to match the sections cut from the light cardboard. Glue this section over the corrugated domed piece so the material is visible through the holes. Glue three punched light cardboard circles on top one another to make radio knobs. You need two knobs. The top of the knobs are made black with a marking pen; then they are glued to the woodtone bank front as indicated on the pattern. This completes the front panel of the bank.

Cover the back panel the same way with woodtone wallpaper. Use your finger to spread glue. A dampened sponge will prove most helpful in removing glue from fingers easily. Provide a bag of dampened sponges in a ziplock plastic bag for classes.

Glue a strip of woodtone wallpaper to the long strip of light cardboard which has the slot tracing on top. The slot is easily cut with a single edge razor blade over a base of thick corrugated cardboard. Fingernail scissors will snip out the corners quickly. For young children, teachers do the slotting.

Glue the bottom corrugated piece between the front and back radio panels. When they are dry, glue around the edges and wrap the long woodtone strip around, starting at the bottom. It is helpful if you wrap this piece around a round glue bottle to precurve it. The last step is to glue a woodtone wallpaper piece to the bottom of the radio.

# Telephone

*Materials needed:*
Light white-faced cardboard
Jesus seal
Corrugated cardboard square ¾" (washer)

¾" paper fastener
18" cotton rug yarn
Fingernail scissors
Ice pick
Sharp single edge razor blade
Paper punch
White glue
Scissors

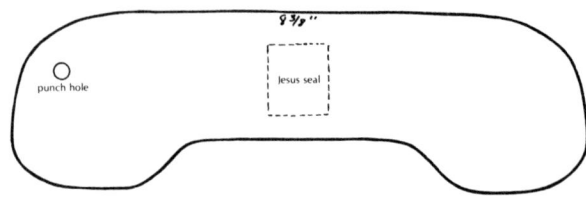

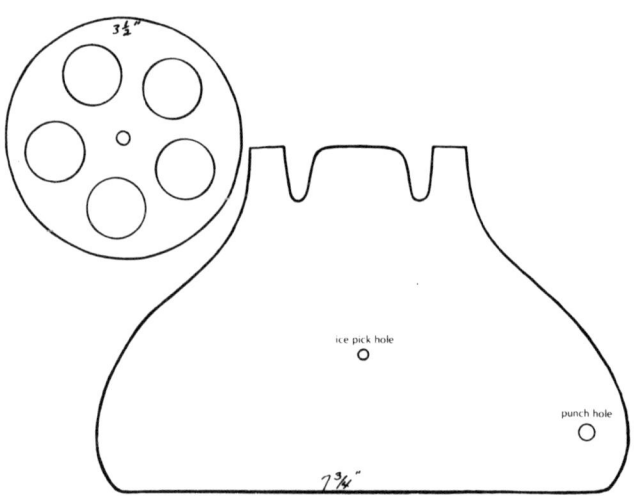

*Assembly:*

Color all the parts after they are cut out. For young ones, you do the cutting, especially the dial holes (with fingernail scissors). The center hole of the dial (for fastener) can be reached through a dial hole. Put some glue on both ends of the yarn and twist. When dry, tie one end to the base and the other to the receiver punched hole. Glue the seal where indicated. Cut the corrugated square and ice pick the hole in the center. Use the razor blade with a sawing motion to cut away the protruding cardboard (washer). The fastener goes through the dial, then washer, then the base. It is flanged carefully on the back of the base. Being loose, it won't squeeze the washer, and the dial will spin freely.

A child can pretend to call a friend and tell him of Jesus by dialing with his finger in the dial holes.

# Game Spinner

**Materials needed:**
  Corrugated cardboard (3″ diameter circle)
  ¾″ paper fastener
  Heavy white construction paper
  Plastic can (orange juice)
  Ice pick
  Pencil
  Scissors
  Paper punch ³/₁₆″
  Black, green, red wide marker
  Electric saber saw with knife-edge blade
  Rubber cement
  Ruler

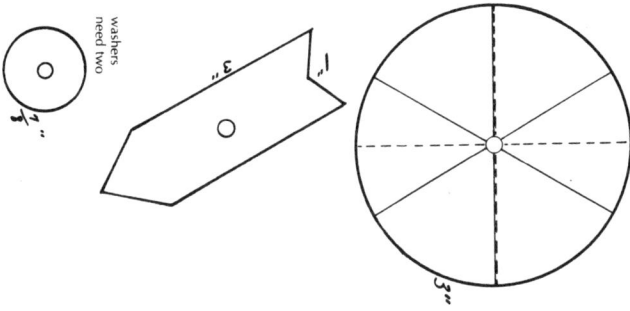

**Assembly:**

Cut corrugated circle with saber saw. Cut another from white construction paper, and a strip ⅛″ x 9⅜″. From the plastic can, cut two strips ¾″ wide, lengthwise to the bottom. From these strips, cut two washers and an arrow. Punch center holes in arrow and washers.

Coat the printed side of the corrugated circle with rubber cement, if it is printed on one side. Coat the edges of the corrugated circle, the white circle, and the long white strip. Allow to dry. You can trace around the corrugated circle onto the white paper and coat the tracing if you have trouble centering the corrugated and white circles. Then trim around the corrugated circle. When cement is dry, put the strip around the corrugated circle and the white circle on top.

Divide the white top into fourths (dotted lines) or sixths (solid lines), marking lightly with a pencil. Color every other space with the red and green marker pens. With the black marker, make separation lines between the colors. Mark numbers in the spaces.

To have a free spinning spinner, it is important you follow the final step carefully. Ice pick a center hole in the corrugated circle as large as possible. Put the fastener through the concave (white) arrow, through the convex (painted) washer, through the corrugated circle, through the convex (painted) washer. Turn the whole spinner over. With opened scissors, as though you were going to cut the fastener, bend the fastener open. Don't put pressure on the washer as you bend the fastener or the arrow won't spin freely. Use this spinner for the "Temple Game," etc.

# Index Card Box

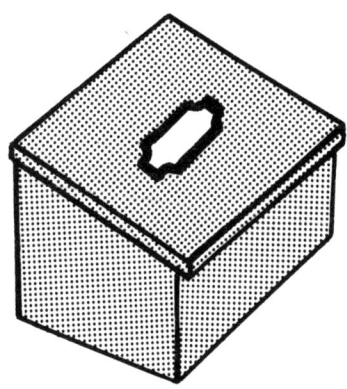

**Materials needed:**
  Corrugated cardboard (lid) 6″ x 5⅛″
  Corrugated cardboard (back) 4½″ x 4¼″
  Corrugated cardboard (floor) 5⅛″ x 4⁹/₁₆″
  Corrugated cardboard (front) 5½″ x 3½″
  Corrugated cardboard (make two sides from pattern)
  3½″ x 1½″ white construction paper (label)
  White glue
  4½″ x 1½″ light white interfacing (hinge)
  Acrylic paint, wallpaper, etc. (to cover outside of box)
  Electric saber saw with knife-edge blade

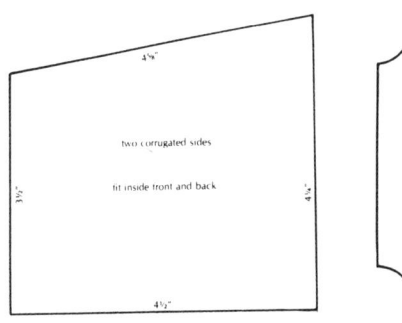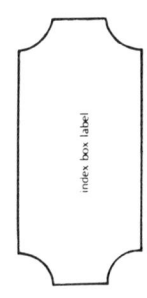

*Assembly:*

Glue the pieces together thus—the sidepieces are glued between the front and back panels. The bottom fits inside all four sides. The lid has ¼" overlap on front and both sides. The back of the box and lid are flush. Spread glue with your finger on top the box, press the hinge onto it, and bring half the hinge down the back, spreading glue with your finger. It makes no difference that glue goes beyond the hinge.

If you elect to paint the box, cover all exposed edges with glue or glue a strip of narrow wallpaper or construction paper on them. Don't use a paper as thin as typing paper! You'll have wavy designed edges.

This box is deeper than the standard index file box for 3" x 5" cards, so it'll handle more cards. You can make your own tab dividers from light cardboard or file folders.

# Secret Decoder

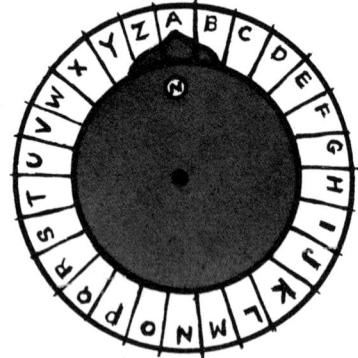

*Materials needed:*

6½" x 6½" white-faced light cardboard
5½" x 5½" light cardboard
Narrow black marking pen
¼" paper punch
Colored construction paper 5½" x 5½" or colored adhesive back paper
½" paper fastener
Ice pick
Sharp single edge razor blade
Ruler
Scissors
Pencil
Rubber cement

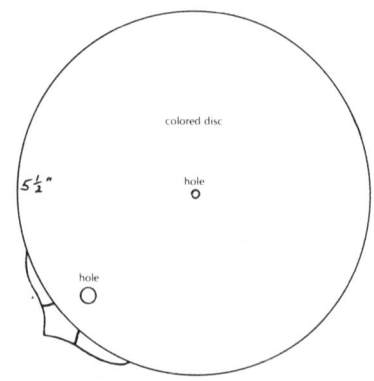

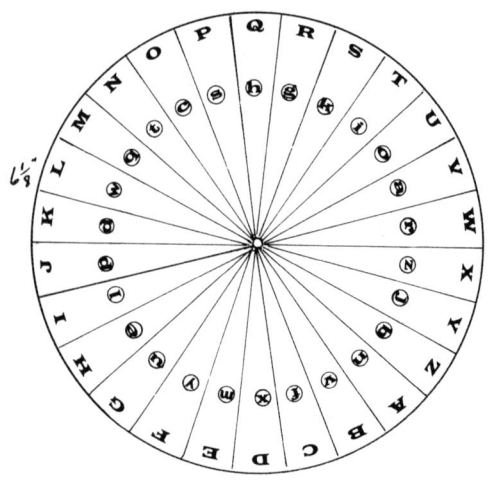

*Assembly:*

Coat the colored paper and the 5½" square of cardboard each on one side with rubber cement. When dry, join the cemented sides carefully. On the back of the cardboard, trace the smaller disc. Mark the pointer marks as pattern shows. Turn over and trace the two holes, after cutting around the outside of the disc. From the colored side, paper punch the hole closest to the outside. With an ice pick, punch through the smaller center hole. Turn it over. Use the razor blade in a sawing motion to cut off the protruding cardboard.

The larger disc pattern has holes marked all around the inner dial. Make a pattern of cardboard and mark the holes on the pattern, then punch them out. By having holes in a pattern, it is easy to trace them onto the white face of the cardboard disc. However, the white cardboard does not have the holes punched out. These are only tracings where the letters are put. You will use them in your coded messages to the children. These letters will be mixed up. Mark the center hole and the line markings around the outside of the disc. Remove the pattern and punch the center hole with the ice pick as you did the smaller disc. Use a ruler to mark the lines from the outer marks to the center hole. With the marking pen, also put the proper letters between the lines close to the edge.

Put a paper fastener through the colored disc, then the white lettered disc, then open it behind. You can give your class Scripture texts to look up during the week by using the mixed-up letters in the punched holes. The child turns to the letter on the inner dial. Then the child finds the right letter on the edge of the larger dial to spell out the secret message. (In a message print any numbers, as they are not in the decoder.)

(Example: From the circled letters on the inner dial _ _ _ _  _ _  _ _ _ _ _ [1 John 1:5]
U C X L K  W L U E I
decoded is "God is light.")

# Finger Puppets

*Materials needed:*
  1" square black felt for each puppet
  6" x 3" red felt
  6" x 3" blue felt
  Two tall pulp egg carton peaks or pattern of light cardboard
  Two one inch Styrofoam balls
  Four glue on ⅛" diameter moving eyes
  Two Styrofoam pellets (used in beanbag furniture)
  1" x ⅞" long yellow fake fur
  1" x ⅞" short brown fake fur
  Two pony tail rubber bands
  Light cardboard
  ⅜" diameter red dried flower with ¼" stem intact
  Rubber cement
  White glue
  Thick white glue
  Scissors
  Fingernail scissors
  Single edge razor blade
  Acrylic flesh paint
  ¼" brush
  Toothpicks
  Styrofoam egg carton

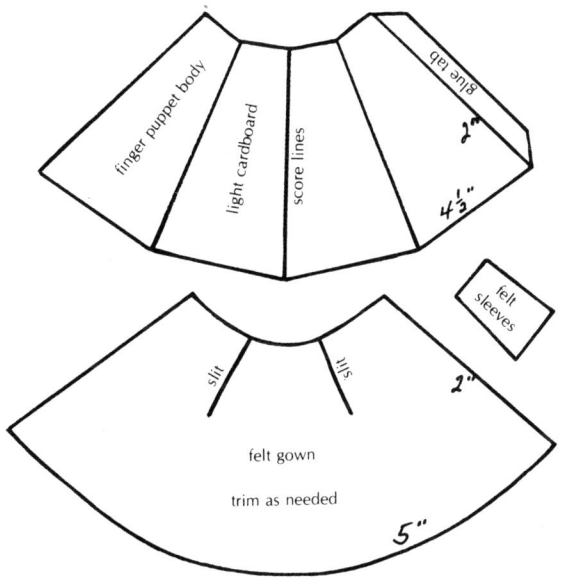

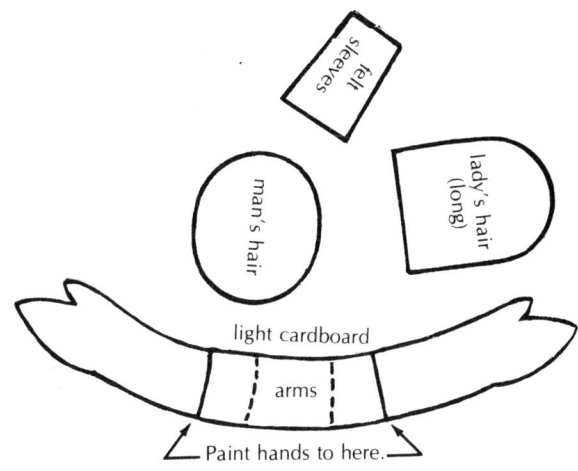

*Assembly:*

If you can't obtain pulp egg cartons for puppet bodies, make them from light cardboard, using the pattern. Trace all patterns and cut them out from materials indicated. Cut a slice from each Styrofoam head (balls) as large as you desire. Coat the inside of the cut section with white glue and press a folded square of black felt into it, which is now the inside of the puppet's mouth. With fingernail scissors, carefully trim the black felt around the edges so it matches the opening. Cut a tongue from red felt and glue it on the section you will use for the puppet's lower mouth. Put a toothpick in the head. Leave the narrow end in the head. Put the larger piece into a Styrofoam egg carton for drying after you have painted the heads. You can make holes in the egg carton with an ice pick or a darning needle. Paint the head with flesh paint. Also paint both sides of the cardboard hand section to a little beyond the hand. You can use the lid of the egg carton to hold the hands for drying. Make slices with a razor blade and stick the unpainted part of the arms into them.

If you cannot find Styrofoam pellets, you can cut a tiny piece from a Styrofoam cup, nose shaped. With a razor blade, cut a very tiny piece from one side of the pellet. Put a dot of glue just above the upper mouth and put the pellet in the glue. Just above the nose, and to either side of it, put two dots of glue and set the eyes in them. When the nose is dry, paint it with flesh paint to match the face.

In cutting the fake fur, it is very important to cut only the cloth backing and not through the hair. With rubber cement, coat the back (cloth side) of the fake fur pieces and the Styrofoam heads where the hair will be placed. Allow to dry, then put the fur to the heads. Rubber cement can be easily rubbed off when it's dry.

Arms are scored on both sides, dotted lines on one side and solid lines on the opposite side. Fold the scored lines, glue the center section and the two smaller sections on either side of the body with white glue. Place it very near the top of the cone body. Move the arms both straight ahead and put a tiny rubber band around them to dry. Remove the rubber band after the arms dry.

When gluing the body covering, start at the front, spreading white glue from the front to the arms, which you carefully pull to an opened side position. Glue one section at a time, overlapping in the back. Cut four felt arm pieces for each puppet and glue them to both the front and back of the arms. Snip the gown where needed. Put a large dot of glue on the top of the bodies. If a cardboard cone is made, glue around the top of the cone liberally. Slice a small section with a razor blade from each head and set the head into the glued body. Put a dot of thick glue at the side and close to the top of the girl's hair. Gently push the dried flower into the glue until the flower rests against the head. Cut the girl's hair so it isn't below her gown.

# Church Bank

Materials needed:
    Corrugated cardboard (floor) 5⅝" x 2"
    Corrugated cardboard (front and back) 6" x 6"
    Light cardboard (roofs and end section)
        11¹³⁄₁₆" x 2⅜"
    White construction paper (stained glass front panel) 2" x 2½"
    Brown or woodtone wallpaper (doors)
        1¼" x 1¼"
    Colored construction paper for windows
    Scissors
    Electric saber saw with knife-edge blade
    Ruler
    Single edge razor blade
    Acrylic paint in two colors (roof and sides)
    ¼" brush
    White glue
    Wide or narrow marking pens of several colors
        (stained window panel)
    Gold cross (optional)
    Chenille cross (optional)

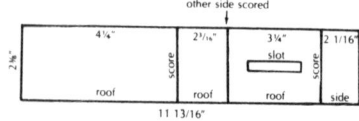

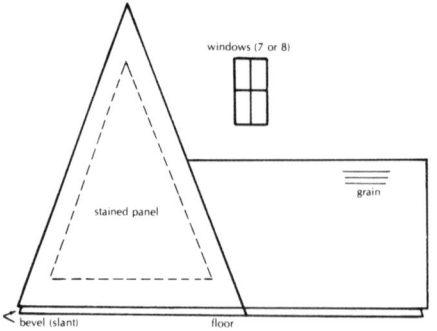

Assembly:
Cut all pieces from materials indicated. Score lightly the fold lines on the roof as indicated in illustration. Cut the slot for the coins with a razor blade. Watch pattern carefully to see which scored line is on the opposite side from the other two.

Bevel the one narrow end of the corrugated floor so it will fit snugly against the peaked portion. To bevel, measure back from the edge ⅛" (printed side). Cut through with the single edge razor blade, only one thickness. With the razor blade turned sharp side up, keep the top of the blade following along the cut line and the other edge of the razor blade along the lower edge of the corrugated bevel. Use a sawing motion and carefully cut the bevel.

Keeping this bevel to your left, glue the floor between the front and back corrugated pieces. The longest measurement is on the bottom. Glue along both short ends and both lengths of the light cardboard scored piece and place it against the corrugated pieces. This forms the whole shell of the bank. If the corrugated parts are in too far, pull them out with the aid of an ice pick or razor blade.

Paint the bank. While it is drying, make your stained glass panel and windows with colored pens. Glue the doors and windows in place, the cross on the colored panel. If desired, the cross of chenille can be put on the roof. Pierce a hole with an ice pick, put a dot of glue on the chenille cross, and push through the hole. If you elect to have the cross on the roof, you may not want one on the stained glass panel.

# Girl's Purse

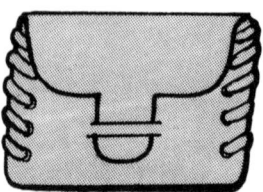

Materials needed:
    Cloth-backed wallpaper or oilcoth 10" x 5"
    A tacky glue

Colored cotton rug yarn (two pieces 12″ long)
Fingernail scissors
Scissors
³/₁₆″ paper punch
White glue

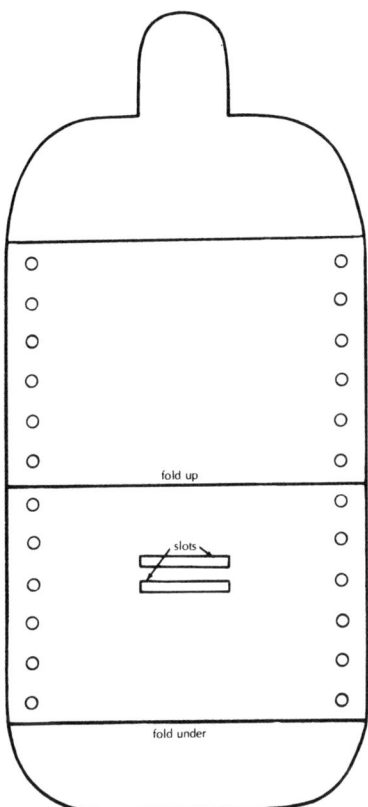

# Crooked Shack

*Materials needed:*
    Corrugated cardboard
    Light cardboard
    Poster paints
    Wide and narrow bristle brushes
    Very lightweight interfacing (5″ x 1″)
    White glue
    Yellow construction paper
    White construction paper and crayons (optional)
    Black marking pen
    Pencil
    Scissors
    Single edge razor blade
    Electric saber saw with knife-edge blade

*Assembly:*

Trace the pattern on the wrong side (cloth) of wallpaper. Cut out and punch holes where indicated. Use fingernail scissors to cut slits where indicated (1/16″ x 1¼″). Glue both ends of the yarn with white glue and twist to form a needle. Glue the other ends to the inside of the bottom of the purse. (This can be done before you give it to the child.) The child can fold over the one edge of the purse and glue it down with a tacky glue and hold it down until it will hold by itself. Repunch any holes covered by the flap foldover. The yarn should be brought to the designed side of the purse before stitching begins.

Whip stitch up both sides of the purse. Leave about ½″ to ¾″ yarn to glue, before cutting the needle end. Glue this end against either side of the purse where the stitching is (inside). Bring the top of the purse down and put the tab fastener through both slits to hold. If the material is rather plain, you can use gummed stickers to decorate by putting rubber cement onto different areas of the purse. Allow to dry. Then peel off the backing of the sticker and apply to the dry cemented area with finger pressure. Rub off any excess rubber cement around the sticker.

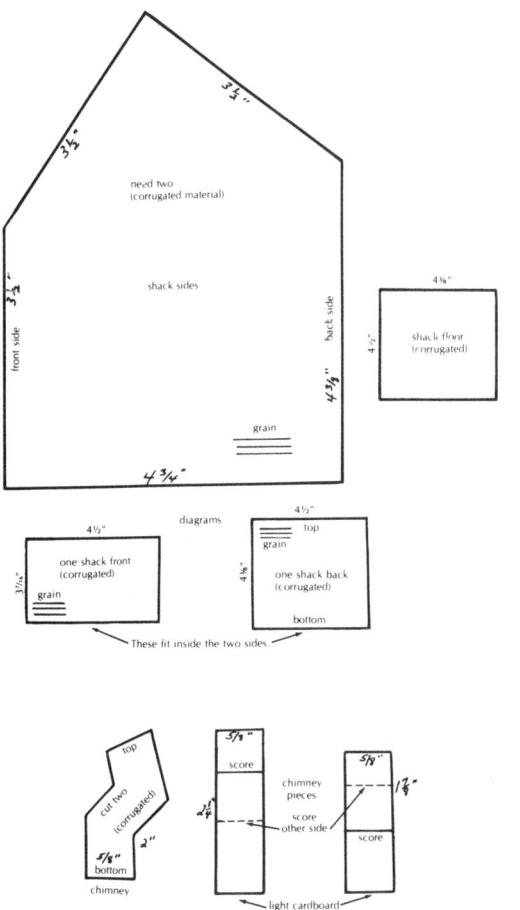

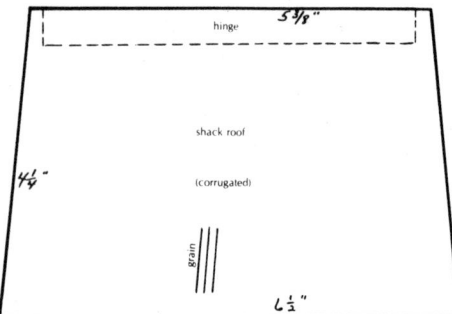

*Assembly:*

At all times, any printing on the cardboard will be to the inside of the shack, because paint won't cover printing.

Trace all patterns onto either corrugated or light cardboard, as patterns indicate. Cut them out. A saber saw with knife-edge blade works very well with corrugated cardboard, producing very straight, smooth edges. Score the chimney pieces where indicated, being careful to score on the side indicated in the pattern (depends on which direction the piece will be bent). Lay the corrugated chimney piece on the table. Glue the bent cardboards to the side they fit. Let it dry. You'll come back to this later to glue the other corrugated part between the two pieces of light cardboard to make the chimney complete.

You will lay the odd shaped shack sides on the table so they are opposite sides up. Glue along both sides of each piece (different lengths) and let them dry a few seconds. You have glued close to the edges and on top the two pieces. Be careful on this step that you haven't glued the wrong sides. Set the sidepiece on one of the odd shaped pieces, close to the edge. Set the other sidepiece on the same piece, close to the edge. Since this is a precision project, it must be glued carefully.

Set the other odd shaped piece on top, matching the edges. You can use bits of masking tape to help hold them while assembling. Are the bottom edges even all around?

Go back to your unfinished chimney and glue along both angled edges of the corrugated piece. Carefully slip it between the two light cardboard sides, so it is flush on both sides. Let it dry.

Now carefully set the shack upright. Glue all around the floor edges. Slip it on an angle down inside, from the top, until it rests squarely at the bottom within the four walls. You can carefully tap it down with the aid of a pencil. If there are any gaps, fill them with glue.

The smallest roof piece is the one that is to the back (tallest) side of the shack and will be glued to a stationary place. Run glue on the three edges of the shack (back and two peaked roof sides). Set the roof section on so that the overhang on the back and both sides is even. This section of roof only comes to the peak, no further. It's on this section of roof you will later glue the chimney.

Cut the hinge piece and glue along the top of the roof, spreading the glue thinly with your finger. Leave half the hinge hanging free. It will be glued later to the other section of roof.

The chimney is marked "top" and "bottom." Glue the edges of the bottom and set on the roof. You can put it anywhere, but NOT on the hinge. If you hold it in place a little bit, it will hold itself until it's fully dry. The top of the chimney has corrugated holes exposed. Run the glue from the bottle along these holes so they are covered by a thin layer. When this has dried, you can paint over the dried glue and give it a more finished appearance. Finish the edges of each roof piece the same way. Let dry.

Cut crooked windows of yellow construction paper, or white if you are going to make crayoned curtains. Cut strips of woodtone wallpaper so the grain runs the longest direction. Strips should be ⅜" wide. Cut a door of woodtone wallpaper, or you can cut it from white construction paper and color it with crayons. Glue the woodtone strips around all four sides of windows and three sides of the door. With a black marking pen, you can add "nails" at both ends of a wood piece. Number the windows and hold them to the shack to trace around them. Put the number on the window you trace, so you will know where each one goes. Do the same with the door.

Glue along the roof top (shortest span opposite the longest span) and lay it on the roof. Spread the glue thinly, as you did before, and bring the hinge down into the glue. If you don't use too much glue, it will dry quickly and hold alone in a short time.

Paint the shack with poster paint, except the windows and door tracings. Glue won't stick to poster painted areas. Paint the roof a contrasting color, when the sides are dry, so the two colors won't mix. Carefully paint the chimney red, brown, or gray.

Glue windows and door in place after the paint has thoroughly dried.

(Application: Your life, as a Christian, should be lived as Jesus lived and taught. It is not to be lived haphazardly, as this shack seems to be built. Crooked dealings are not for the Christian. We are to live each day as though it were our last on earth. This shack can be used as a crayon box or a storage box.)

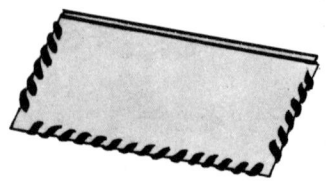

# Wallet

*Materials needed:*
    Cloth-backed wallpaper or oilcloth 9″ x 8½″
    Cloth-backed wallpaper or oilcloth 4″ x 3″
    A tacky glue
    Colored cotton rug yarn 29″
    Scissors
    ³⁄₁₆″ paper punch
    White glue

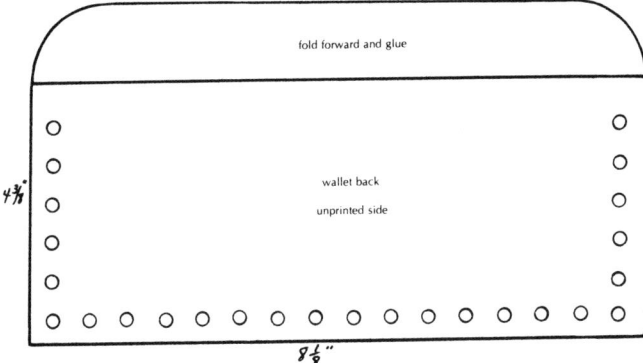

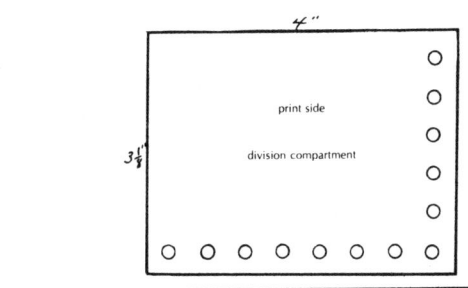

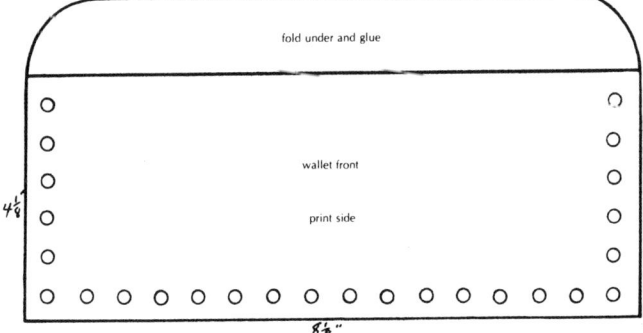

*Assembly:*

Trace the patterns on the cloth side of wallpaper and cut out. Punch holes as marked. Glue one end of the yarn with white glue and twist to form a short needle. Allow to dry. Glue the flaps down with evenly spread tacky glue. Hold down until it will hold alone. Place parts thus: back of wallet with cloth side up, the division compartment to the far right with the design side up (holes aligned), the front of the wallet with the design side up (holes aligned). You will need to repunch some of the top holes where the foldover covers them.

Glue the free end of the yarn to the inside of the

wallet along the punched holes. Bring the needle yarn out the top punched hole, around the back, and through the same hole again. Whip stitch all around the edge, ending with a leftover piece ½″ to ¾″. Cut the rest off. Glue the yarn end to the inside of the wallet, very close to the punched holes. The division is free on two sides, so the child can put folded notes, etc. and keep them separate from his paper money. You might give him a few bills of paper money for his wallet. If you put a seal of Jesus on one of the paper bills, you could turn this into a "tithing" project, to show that some of the child's money belongs to God.

# Palm Tree

*Materials needed:*
    Green crepe paper 25″ x 3¾″
    Brown construction paper 9″ x 6″
    Pencil
    White glue
    Electric saber saw with knife-edge blade
    Corrugated cardboard 2″ x 2″
    Artificial grass (used in model trains)
    Scissors

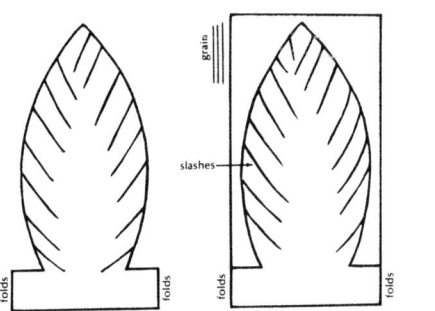 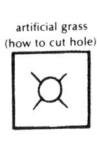

*Assembly:*

Fold the crepe paper end over and every two inches for 12 folds. The grain (lines) of crepe should run the length of the leaf. Cut leaf as in illustration. Carefully pull it apart. (Leaves are in a long string.) Wind the base of the leaves around a pencil and glue end seam. Carefully remove from the pencil and set aside.

Wind the brown paper on a pencil, having one

end larger than the other. Remove it from the pencil and let it unwind slightly. Then with a dot of glue on the corner, glue to hold together. If trunk isn't long enough, pull it a little from both ends. Cut up the widest end in four places about ½" to ¾". Cut these slits off square. Fan these tabs out.

Cut a hole in a square of artificial grass that is a little larger than the corrugated base for the trunk to fit into. Glue a long narrow strip of artificial grass to go around the base. Put glue on the top of the tabs of the trunk. Bring the square of artificial grass down over the trunk to rest on these tabs. Press all tabs to the underneath part of the grass. Glue the tops of the corrugated base and bring the trunk with grass down onto it. Trim around the grass as needed.

Cut a tiny ear off the top of the tree trunk. Glue around the base and the edges of the roll (so they won't unwind). Insert the leaves in the hole of the top trunk. Spread and twist the leaves until you get the desired appearance.

These make nice additions to a Biblical scene or table decoration.

# Candlestick

*Materials needed:*
  Corrugated cardboard 3" x 3"
  Electric saber saw with knife-edge blade
  Woodtone wallpaper
  Ruler
  Scissors
  #14 Ditalini macaroni (68 pieces)
  White glue
  Gold enamel (airplane type)
  One 12" yellow chenille wire (cut to 7" and 3½" pieces)
  One 6" yellow chenille wire (cut to 4½" and 2½" pieces)
  Three flat toothpicks
  Narrow black marker pen
  Ice pick
  White acrylic paint (candles)
  Small paint brush
  Two 12" chenille wires or straws (narrow plastic)

*Assembly:*
  Cut the four chenille wire pieces into the right sizes with scissors or wire cutters. Bend the 7", 4½", and 2½" pieces in half. The marks on the 3½" upright chenille wire is where the other three bent chenille wire pieces will be twisted. Start at the top and twist (only one twist) the smallest (2½") wire on the mark ½" down from the top. Put two beads of macaroni on from the bottom. Next comes the 4½" bent wire and three beads below it. Next comes the bent 7" wire and four beads below it.

String all the other beads of macaroni on chenille wires to paint with gold enamel, or on a narrow slit plastic straw stuck in a pierced hole on an egg carton. Paint the macaroni and allow to dry thoroughly. Also paint the beads on the upright chenille wire.

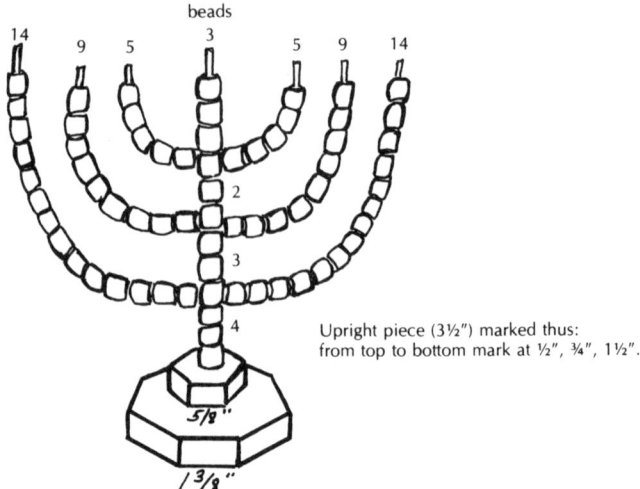

Upright piece (3½") marked thus:
from top to bottom mark at ½", ¾", 1½".

Cut the corrugated pieces and glue two small ones together and two large ones together. If you cut two layers together, the pieces will match. Glue a strip of wallpaper around the edges of both double layers (glued together) of both pieces. Glue traced wallpaper coverings to the tops of both pieces. Trim as needed. Use very little glue, spreading it with your finger. Center the small piece on the larger one and glue them together. Pierce the smallest piece in the center with the ice pick. Put some glue on the chenille upright (below the four beads) and stick it into this hole.

Cut toothpicks into ⅜" to ½" pieces. Discard the thicker parts of the toothpicks (seven candles). When the macaroni beads are dry, string them on the arms and bend the arms in arcs upward so all are even at the top. Put a dot of glue in the top bead and slip a candle in the edge. When dry, paint the candles white.

(Larger types of these candlesticks were used in Hebrew homes.)

# Swiss Chalet

*Materials needed:*

Electric saber saw with knife-edge blade

Ruler

Light cardboard (bay window and chimney)

Corrugated cardboard (roof) 10″ x 8″ (scored so two sides are 5″ x 8″)

Corrugated cardboard (first floor bottom) 5″ x 5″

Corrugated cardboard (second floor bottom) 6″ x 7½″ (1½″ x 6″ is deck area)

Corrugated cardboard (two ends of second floor)

Corrugated cardboard (two second floor sides fit inside two peaked ends)

Corrugated cardboard (first floor sides fit inside two ends) 4⁹/₁₆″ x 3″

Corrugated cardboard (two first floor ends) 4⅞″ x 3″

Corrugated cardboard (deck railing) 1″ x 6¹/₁₆″

Corrugated cardboard (two deck railings) 1″ x 1⅜″

Lightweight white interfacing (hinge) 1½″ x 7⅞″

Acrylic paint for chimney, first floor, second floor, roof

¼″ brush

Gift wrap or seed catalog with small flowers in color

Narrow black marking pen

White glue

Scissors

Yellow construction paper (nine small windows) 1″ x ¾″

Yellow construction paper (bay window) 2⅜″ x ⅞″

Yellow construction paper (front, second floor window series) 5″ x 2″

Yellow construction paper (rear, second floor window series) 5″ x 3″

Woodtone wallpaper (side door, bay window roof, bottom, and trim, window series)

Woodtone wallpaper (front, first floor panel) 3³/₁₆″ x 2¼″

Construction paper (colored, front first floor door) 1⅜″ x 1⅞″

Black construction paper (two railing strips for top and bottom) 3/₁₆″ x 9¼″

Black construction paper (eighteen window shutters) ¾″ x ½″

Black construction paper (twelve railing crossbar strips) 1⅝″ x ⅛″

Black construction paper (railing upright strips) 3/₁₆″ x ⅞″

Small paint brush

*Assembly:*

This project has storage in the top floor. The bottom floor is hollow. Cut all pieces from cardboard, etc. Start construction with the first floor. You don't want a corrugated edge showing from the front of the chalet except for the floor pieces.

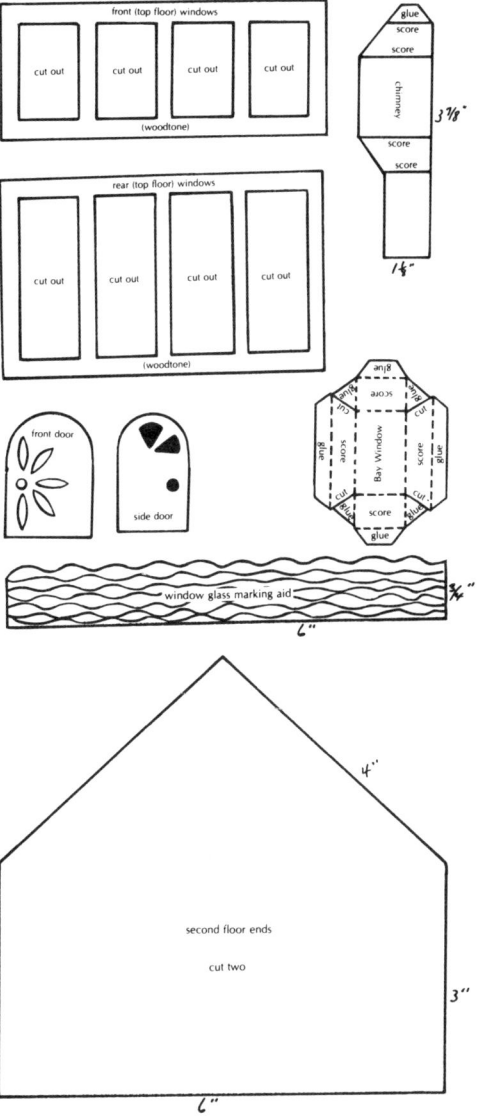

Glue the first floor sides inside the two first floor ends to form the shell of the first floor. Glue around the top edge of the floor piece and set the sides shell on top the glue, squaring it. The end piece is the one to be the front of the chalet.

Glue the second floor on top the first floor section. There will be about a half inch overhang on the three sides and about two inches overhang in the front. On the second story floor glue the two sides inside the two peaked ends to form a shell. Glue this shell to the floor, keeping it even with the back of the floor piece. (This allows for a desk in the front.) Glue the scored roof (cut in half on the scored line) to the left side of the peaked front so it has even overhangs on three sides (none at the peak). Set the other half of the roof on, matching pieces. Glue the hinge from the glued roof section onto the unglued roof section, spreading glue with your finger. Glue the chimney together. Paint the chimney and allow it to dry.

Glue the long corrugated railing to the front of the deck. Glue the two smaller railings between the long railing and the front of the second story wall. Glue all exposed corrugated edges and let dry.

Paint the first floor one color, the second floor another color, except the deck area. (Railings are white.) Paint the second story deck floor the same color as the second story sides. Paint the roof. Paint the top of the corrugated railing black. Glue one long black paper strip along the top of the railing and the other along the bottom of it. The front of the railing has four sections and one section on each side. On the short sides, glue one short black upright strip at each end. On the front railing, glue one short black upright at each end and three others evenly spaced between. The crossbars form an X between each upright, so there are four X sections in the front of the deck railing.

Form the bay window, glue yellow construction paper to the three sides, a woodtone piece to the roof and underneath part, and two small strips on each winged side to divide the windows. Use the marking aid to make the wavy lines on all window pieces before you glue them, using a narrow black marking pen. Cut the window series from woodtone and glue over the windows (yellow construction paper).

Glue the woodtone panel to the front first floor, far left. The front door is glued to the right. It can be decorated with crayons, marking pens, etc. A small window is glued on the woodtone panel and black shutters are glued to the sides of the window. Glue the smaller window series just above the top of the railing, centering it on the peaked front of the second story. Glue the smaller woodtone door to rest on the ground. The larger window series goes on the peaked second story rear.

The model has two tiny windows on both sides of the second story, two on the back of the first story, one small window and one bay window on the first story right, one small window and one small door on the first story left. Glue flowers along the sides of the first story. You can also add them to the back wall of the deck area.

Glue around the chimney edge and set it on the roof (glued part) to your left. You can add more glue to the inside, spreading it on the edges with a toothpick.

# Church Storage Box

*Materials needed:*
   Electric saber saw with knife-edge blade
   Corrugated cardboard 8″ x 6″ (solid peaked roof)
   Corrugated cardboard 8″ x 6″ (cut into two pieces, 8″ x 3″ for other side of peaked roof)
   Corrugated cardboard 7¾″ x 3⅝″ (wing roof)
   Corrugated cardboard 7¾″ x 5⅛″ (peaked section floor)
   Corrugated cardboard 5⅞″ x 3⅛″ (wing floor)
   Corrugated cardboard 3″ x 3⅛″ (wing end)
   Corrugated cardboard 6″ x 5″ (two peaked parts, front and back)
   Corrugated cardboard 7½″ x 6″ x 3″ (two wing sides)
   Very lightweight interfacing (white) 7¼″ x 1½″ (wing hinge)
   Very lightweight interfacing (white) 8″ x 1½″ (peaked hinge)
   Very lightweight interfaciing (white) ½″ x 1½″ (pull tab on peaked section)
   Single edge razor blade
   White glue
   Ruler
   Two colors acrylic paint (root and sides)
   White construction paper (stained glass panel)
   Wide tip marking pens in colors
   Gold cross 1″ to 1½″ long
   Colored construction paper for windows of wing
   Brown construction paper or woodtone wallpaper for doors
   Wide brush ¼″ to ⅜″
   Chenille cross on top church (optional)
   Ice pick (optional)

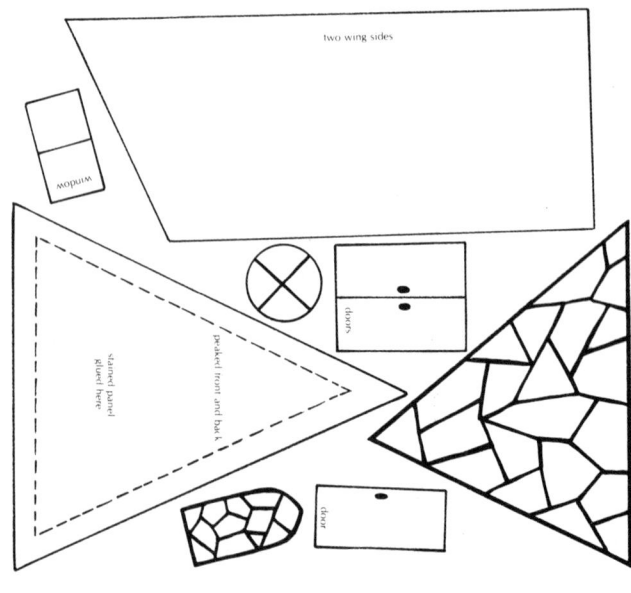

*Assembly:*

Cut all corrugated cardboard pieces with the saber saw. (See introductory pages for directions.) You will need to bevel the short side of the wing roof and the two 7¾" lengths of the peaked floor, if they are to fit well. Bevel by ruling back ⅛" from the edge (printed sides of corrugate). With a razor blade, cut through only the top layer of corrugate, following the ruled line. Turn the razor blade upside down and cut in a sawing motion toward you carefully, so the protruding blade will follow the traced line on top and the lower edge of the razor blade will follow the edge of the lower layer of corrugate. This gives a bevel. All floors fit between all walls. Always keep any printing to the inside of a project, as paint does not cover printing well.

Glue both wing sides to the wing end piece. The end is between the sides. Glue along the lowest point of the inside of the three sides and set the wing floor in. Any gaps can be filled with glue before painting.

Now proceed with the assembling of the peaked section. Glue the peaked sides to the flat surface of the solid roof section, keeping the edges flush. Set it in a standing position to assure the solid roof is setting square with the peaked sides. On the other side, at the bottom of the two peaks, is glued the narrow roof section. Set the upper section in place, but no gluing. The hinge is glued half on one side and half on the solid side, spreading the glue with your finger. The floor is pressed into place between the four walls. Glue around all four walls and press the floor up from the bottom into the glue. Now bring the wing up to the solid roof section of the peaked part. Measure back from the peaked solid roof 2¼". Glue the wing slanted sides and floor and bring it up against the slanted roof. Gaps can be filled with glue before painting.

Set the wing roof on and do the hinge the same way. Spread glue on the hinge on the roof, then bring the hinge down the back of the wing side (no overlap). This roof only has an overlap on two sides. Glue the folded tab to the center of the top section of the peaked roof (to aid opening).

There are two ways to finish the edges. You can glue all holes and gaps shut, then allow to dry before painting, or you can glue strips of wallpaper or construction paper to all exposed edges (thin paper ripples). Fill all gaps with glue and dry before painting.

Cut the large stained glass panel, windows, and doors. You can make stained glass windows in the wing section, too, or plain ones. The double door is in the front and single door in the back. Do your stained glass with marker pens over newspaper thicknesses or a piece of corrugated cardboard. (It often bleeds through.) When all are dry, glue them in place, on the sides of the painted church. Glue a gold cross on the stained glass panel. If you elect to put a chenille cross on the peaked roof, you may not want the gold cross on the stained glass panel.

Pencils can go in the peaked section and crayons in the wing section.

# Picnic Table

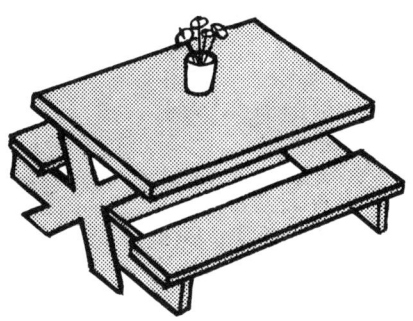

*Materials needed:*

8" x 4½" corrugated cardboard
Electric saber saw with knife-edge blade
White glue
Woodtone wallpaper or acrylic paint
Typing paper 1½" x ½" (vase)
Dowel ¼" diameter or round pencil (for winding vase)
Two round green (painted) toothpicks
Small inch square of colored construction paper (flowers)
Ice pick
Acrylic paint (vase)
¼" paper punch

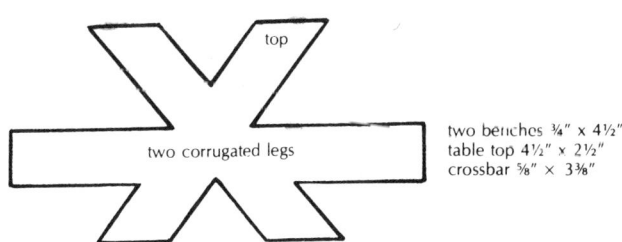

top

two corrugated legs

two benches ¾" x 4½"
table top 4½" x 2½"
crossbar ⅝" × 3⅜"

*Assembly:*

Cut traced pieces from corrugated cardboard with an electric saber saw. Keep all printing facing the inside (toward ground). If you elect to paint the table, cover edges with wallpaper or construction paper first. Wind the typing paper vase around the pencil or dowel so the vase is ½" tall. Glue lightly along the seam and hold a few seconds until dry. Paint.

Glue the table legs crossbar to the same edges of the upper section of the leg pieces. While you are waiting for this to dry, punch four circles from colored paper for flowers. Pierce each in the center

21

with a large pin or the ice pick. Break the round toothpicks into various lengths (discarding the center thicker parts). Place the flowers on the sharp points of the green stems. With a toothpick, apply a very tiny dot of glue to the top of each flower where the stem comes through, so they won't come off.

Lay the table top upside down (printed corrugate up) on a flat working surface. Glue all the four leg tops and place them evently on both ends of the table top. Allow to dry some before setting it upright. Glue the edges where the benches will go on the table legs. Match both benches with the table top so they don't run on a crooked angle.

If you cover with wallpaper, do so before assembly. If you paint, do this after the table is completely assembled and glue is dry. When the table paint is dry, glue around the very edge of the vase and set it onto the center of the table top. Fill the vase with glue about halfway. Set the flower stems in the vase so they look nice.

These make a nice service camp table decoration. You can give them way as awards or door prizes.

# Hidden Compartment Chest

*Materials needed:*
   Corrugated cardboard
   Light cardboard
   Woodtone wallpaper
   White glue
   Two pieces of satin ribbon ¼" x 1¼" long
   Decorations (wallpaper, catalogs, gift wrap, etc.)
   Very lightweight interfacing material 4¾" x 1" (hinge)
   Electric saber saw with knife-edge blade or razor blade
   Scissors
*Pattern dimensions:*
   Corrugated chest front and backs 5" x 2½"
   Corrugated lid 5½" x 3⅛"
   Light cardboard chest bottom 5" x 2⅞"

Corrugated tray front and back are 4½" x 1"
Corrugated tray sides are 2¹/₁₆" x 1"
Light cardboard tray bottom is 4⁹/₁₆" x 2½"
⅛" long strips of woodtone wallpaper for covering exposed edges
15¾" x 2½" woodtone wallpaper will go around chest
Woodtone wallpaper bottom piece is 5" x 3"
Woodtone wallpaper lid pieces (top and bottom) are 5½" x 3⅛"
Corrugated ''stops'' (two pieces) 1¼" x 2³/₁₆"
Corrugated ''stops'' (two pieces) 1¼" x 4⅝"

*Assembly:*
   This chest is fascinating to Juniors, because of the hidden compartment. Nothing can be hidden from God, no matter where you are, or how well you think you have hidden your sins done in secret. Rest assured, God will always know.

Cut all pieces from materials indicated on the pattern dimensions listing. Remember, this is a precision type project. Keep the traced lines on patterns, for it is important you cut straight and don't increase the sizes. In working with children, it is helpful if you label the parts in pencil. It avoids many mistakes in assembling. Also, either place all cut parts in a brown lunch sack or place a rubber band around a complete project's parts for each child. (Explain this craft must have parts glued immediately on the edge of other parts, so everything is always straight. You can use bits of masking tape to hold pieces together until glue dries.)

Two boxes will be assembled. First, the outside box. Run a ribbon of glue along both short sides of the front and back pieces, on top and close to the edges. (The *unprinted* side should be on the outside if the corrugated cardboard has printing on it. Printing will be hidden by the wallpaper.) Let them stand a few seconds, depending upon how humid the weather is. When you look down on the box, you will see exposed edges. These can be covered by gluing strips of wallpaper if you desire. Set the two smaller ends on one of the long glued pieces (one at each end). Are they immediately off the edge? Keep the printing to the *outside*, always. Carefully set the other long piece on top, aligning the edges. Carefully set it upright and run glue along all four edges. Set the chest bottom onto the glue and make sure it's square. After it's dry, you can trim off any light cardboard as needed. Allow to dry.

Now the inner box, or tray, is formed. Any printing on this box is also kept to the outside. Assemble it exactly as you did the larger box.

When it has dried, fold the piece of satin ribbon in half and glue about ⅜" of one end to the outside of a smallest end and the other end of the ribbon to the inside of the tray, so you have ribbon extending in the air to use as a pull. Do the same to the other end of the tray.

Back to the larger box. There are four pieces marked "stops." Put a few dots of glue on the printed sides of these and set them at the inner sides of the large box, against the bottom. Place the smaller end "stops" within the two longer ones, all against the sides and to the bottom of the box. The tray will rest on these stops and hide the lower compartment.

Place the lid on the top of the larger box and glue a hinge on the back, bringing it over onto the lid. Spread the glue thinly with your finger, pressing the hinge into it. The lid overlaps on both sides and front, but is flush in the back. Allow to dry.

Cut decorations from whatever you wish. The hinge can dry as you do this.

Aluminum yardsticks are ideal in craft work for measuring wallpaper strips. Put all seams to the back or one of the back corners. Spread glue with your finger on one side at a time of the large box and put the wallpaper on. Cover the lid, top and underneath, the bottom of the chest, and exposed edges with thin strips of wallpaper. When it's covered, glue on decorations and slip the tray inside. When you pull the tray out, pull both ribbons at the same time or it won't come out.

# BIBLE CRAFTS

## Baptism of Jesus

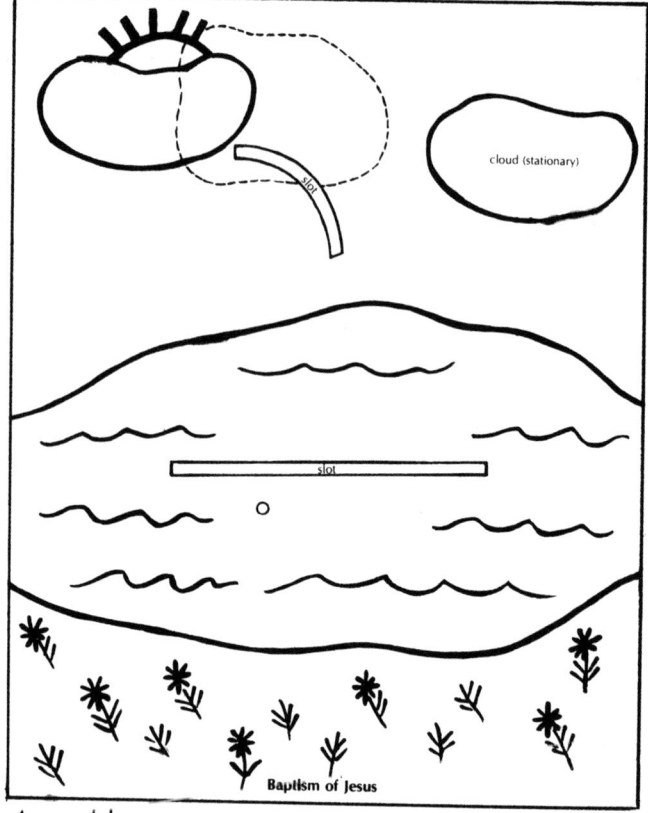

Baptism of Jesus

*Materials needed:*
  White light cardboard (8″ x 10″) for background
  White light cardboard 4″ x 4½″
  Crayons
  Two paper fasteners ½″
  Single edge razor blade
  Wide black marker pen
  Narrow black marker pen
  Ice pick
  ⅛″ hole paper punch
*Variation will need the following:*
  White glue
  Blue construction paper 8″ x 5″
  Two cotton balls
  Scissors

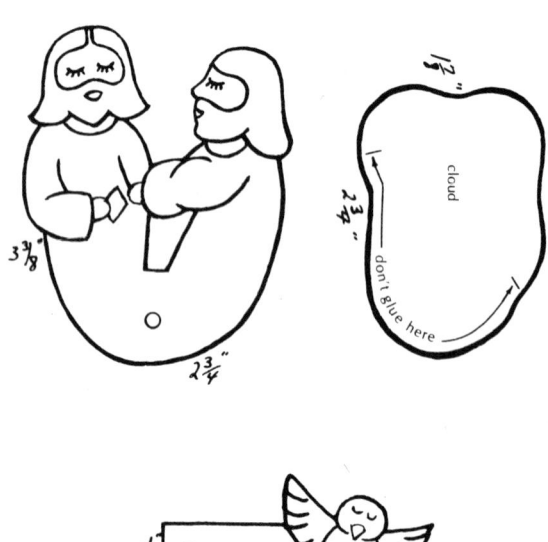

*Assembly:*

If you have access to a duplicating machine, you can have figures and dove (Holy Spirit's form) done. (Otherwise they can be hand drawn.) The dotted lines are for the most difficult variation to be done by older children.

Prepare the background slotting for the water and dove (as indicated on pattern) with a razor blade. Holes for the paper fasteners are made with a paper punch and ice pick. Cut out figures and dove. Make the cloud outlines, water with ripples, and sun with wide black marker pen. With the narrow black marker, at the bottom edge, print either "John Baptizing Jesus" or "Baptism of Jesus." Make sun's rays. Color sun, water, figures, grass, flowers, and stems. The design shows a very simple flower for the young child to draw. Assemble by placing figures into the water, aligning the two holes, and putting a paper fastener through them. Slip the tab of the dove into the slot, align the holes, and put the second paper fastener through.

In the more difficult variation, one cloud is stationary and the other is a separate piece of cardboard. Glue a pulled cottonball to both surfaces. Water is outlined lightly with a pencil, to guide the child in placing the water correctly. When gluing the water, do not glue along the lower edge of the slot in the water. Unglued the figures can be lowered into it. But do glue the top edge of the slot and all around the edge of the water piece. Line the

24

water slots up and press into place on the background. Be careful in gluing the cloud in place on the dotted line. Leave the lower right part free of glue so the dove can be lowered from the cloud. It is hidden from view behind the cloud until the proper time of ascending. (The simple version is best for the young child.)

You can also change the scene by eliminating the dove, dove's slot, punched hole, and having two stationary clouds. By changing the bottom caption to read, "Philip Baptizing the Eunuch," you can use it for that Bible story. (This type of craft is fascinating to children because it does something.)

# Temple Game

*Materials needed:*
8½″ x 11″ white-faced light cardboard
Four penny sized white cardboard discs
Penny for tracing
Crayons
Spinner (in this book)
Scissors
Black narrow marking pen
Ruler

*Assembly:*
Draw the pattern onto white cardboard. Trace around a penny onto white cardboard to get white discs. For thicker discs, glue one on top another. Color board as indicated, decorating with trees, grass, and flowers at random. Draw a temple at the end of the pathway and color it.

You will need to make a spinner from directions in this book on page 11. Spin the arrow and advance as many spaces as the arrow or color indicate. (If you want to use colors instead of numbers, put the four different colors on the spinner and advance to the color that comes up when you spin. Using colors would be better for children who do not know their numbers.)

This is a simple game for four or less young children. The one reaching the temple first wins the game.

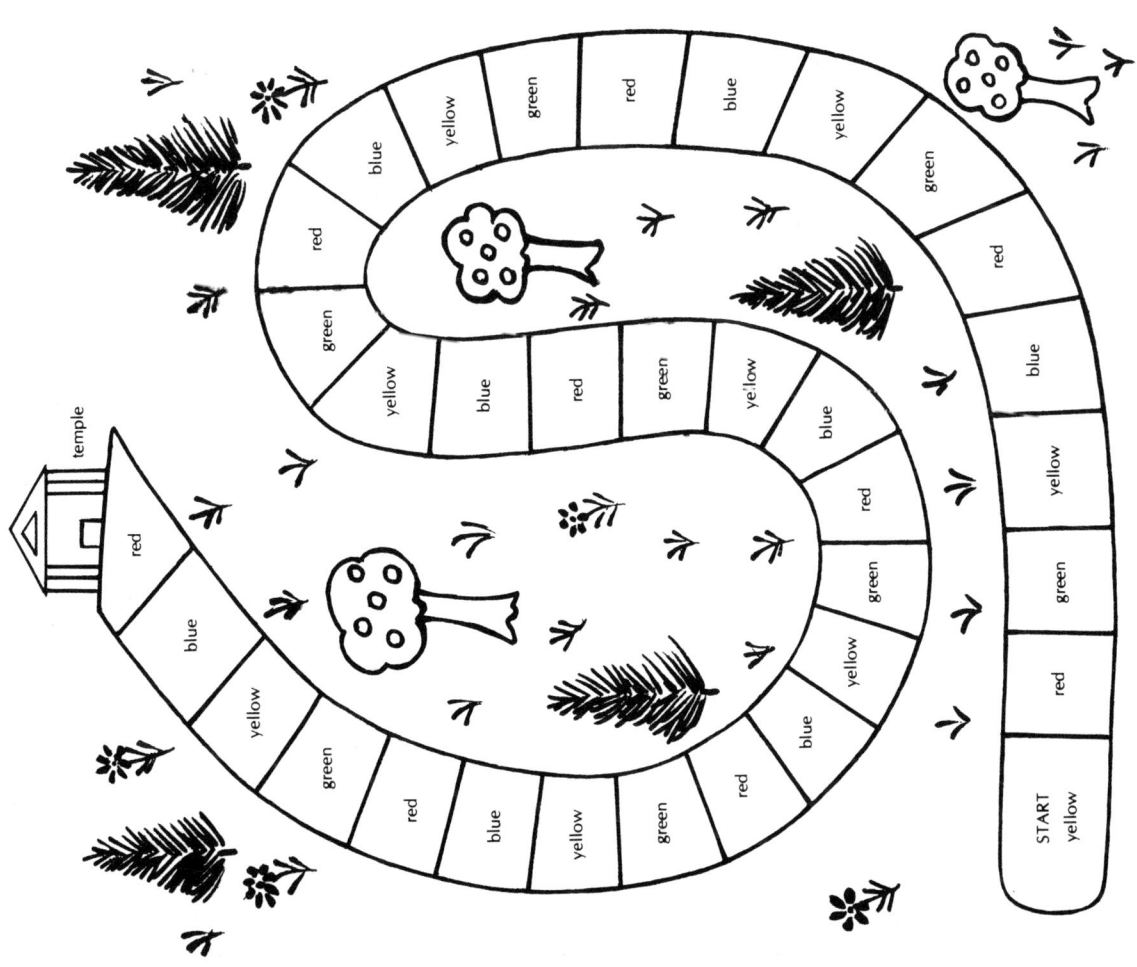

# Pharaoh's Daughter

*Materials needed:*

Pulp egg carton peak (almost 2" tall)
1" molded foam ball (not Styrofoam)
Two pieces blue chenille wire (arms)
3" black chenille wire (fan)
Two fluffy red feathers cut to 1½" lengths (fan)
One #14 Ditalini macaroni (bead) for fan
Acrylic paints in flesh, black, and blue
¼" brush
Gold airplane enamel
Small brush
A tacky glue
Ice pick
⅛" paper punch
Scissors
Black and red marking pens (narrow)
Yellow construction paper (headband)

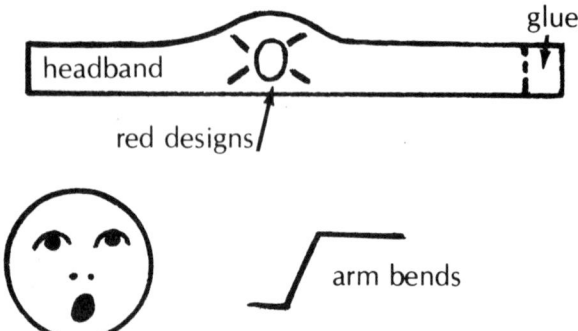

facial features

*Assembly:*

Cut peaks from egg cartons with a lot of excess pulp around them. Look from the inside of the peak, set the blade of your scissors across two low points on the corners, and cut straight across. Do this with all four sides. Trim slightly if it doesn't set level on a flat surface. Put a large dot of glue on top the peak and set the ball into it. Let dry. Cut two feathers to length and trim to rounds if necessary.

Put a dot of glue on the end of the black chenille wire. Slip the macaroni bead just over the top of the wire, so it's at the top of the bead head. Put another dot of glue into the bead hole. Stick the feathers along the side so they fan outwards. Put a dot of glue around the feathers if they don't have enough to secure them after you've pushed them in. Let it dry some by propping it on the edge of a box, etc.

Cut the blue chenille wire to lengths and bend as illustrated. The smallest section is the hand. Go back to the head and paint the face area with flesh paint. Paint the body cone blue. Clean brushes in water.

With the small brush, paint the macaroni bead below the feathers with gold enamel. Clean brush immediately in solvent. Prop it up to dry, or stick it in an egg carton which has a hole pierced with an ice pick.

Cut headband from yellow construction paper, overlap it about ¼", and glue. Roll it around your finger to give it a curve before gluing. Hold it until it will stick alone.

When the face is dry, paint black hair on the head. Pierce a hole on each side up 1¼" from the bottom. Do the piercing with an ice pick. Her left arm is extended upwards and her right arm down. When sticking the arms into the pierced holes, put a dot of glue on the arm and stick it into the hole. Later, when they have dried, you can bend her right arm to her side.

Now punch a hole ⅛" up from the bottom of the body on her left side. Put a dot of glue on the bottom end of the black fan. Stick it into the punched hole. Put another dot of glue on the front of her hand and press the black wire against it. Hold or prop it until it will hold alone. When it dries, you can add more glue if needed to secure it. When the hair has dried, you can set the headband on her head by using three or four dots of glue close to the band on the inside. When her face is thoroughly dry, you can add the facial features with red and black markers.

# Jesus Pendant

*Materials needed:*

Two "The Christ" seals, #1943 (Standard Publishing)
Two acetate ovals 2" x 1½"
One smaller oval 1" x 1½" white construction paper
33" piece of colored yarn
⅛" paper punch
Masking tape
White glue
Scissors

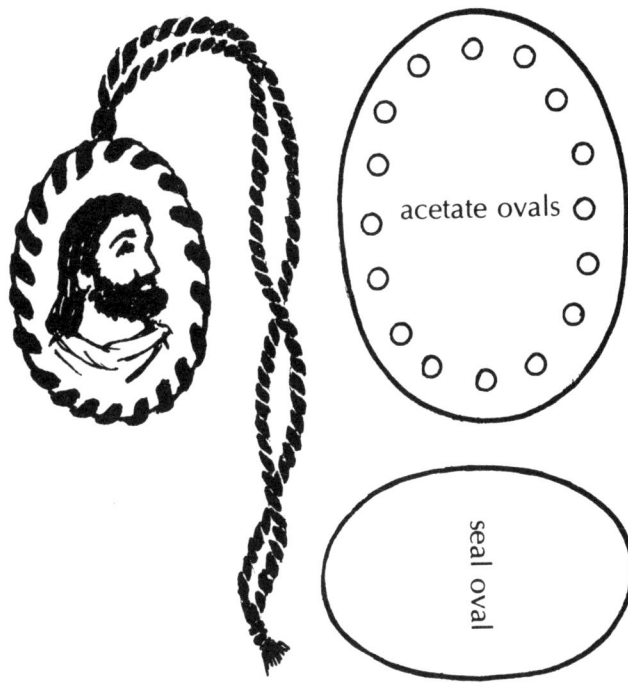

⅛" moving eye
Narrow black marking pen
White glue
Scissors

*Assembly:*

Trace and cut out all pieces. Draw outline lines with a black marking pen. Color all pieces except the glue space on the leg of Jesus. Glue this space lightly and add to the back of the Jesus figure. Glue the moving eye on the donkey. Jesus slips on the donkey with one leg over the back of the donkey. Add flowers, tress, etc. as you wish.

*Assembly:*

If the child has a large head, add two inches to the yarn length. Put two pieces of acetate together. Place the pattern (light cardboard) on top. Put a tiny piece of masking tape on either side to hold all together, but don't press the masking tape down. Cut around the oval pattern. Then punch the holes very carefully (so you don't ruin your pattern). Remove one of the bits of masking tape.

Put a dot or two of white glue on one end of the string. Twist to form a short needle. Cut the seals to fit within the white construction paper oval. Glue one to each side. (Or you could put a red heart on one side indicating, "My heart belongs to Jesus.") Slip the picture oval down from the bottom, top, or side, so all punched holes are free. A sharp pencil will aid this process. Carefully remove the other bit of masking tape without shifting the acetate holes. (Now you can put a paper clip up from the bottom. Remove it when you come to it in stitching.)

Start at the top center hole. Leave 12" (13" if larger head) of the yarn before beginning the whip stitching around the pendant. When you come up to the starting top hole, go into it from the opposite side. Tie a knot close to the pendant with both strings. Tie another knot close to the end and cut off the glued part.

# Jesus on Donkey

*Materials needed:*
    7" x 7" white-faced light cardboard or construction paper
    Crayons

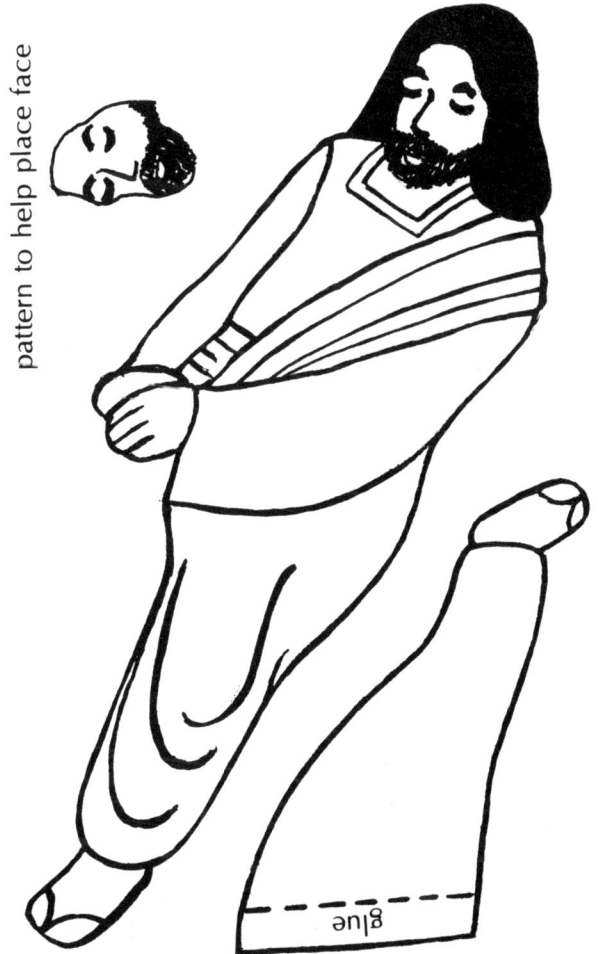

pattern to help place face

glue

# King Saul

Materials needed:
- Frozen juice can (plastic)
- Corrugated 3″ diameter circle
- Electric saber saw with knife-edge blade
- Lightweight white interfacing (hinge) 1″ x ¾″
- Light cardboard (crown) 1″ x 2½″
- Gold or yellow construction paper (crown covering) 1″ x 2½″

hinge

corrugated lid

cut one

cut out X's

set in center of lid

crown

glue this edge

match points and glue overlap

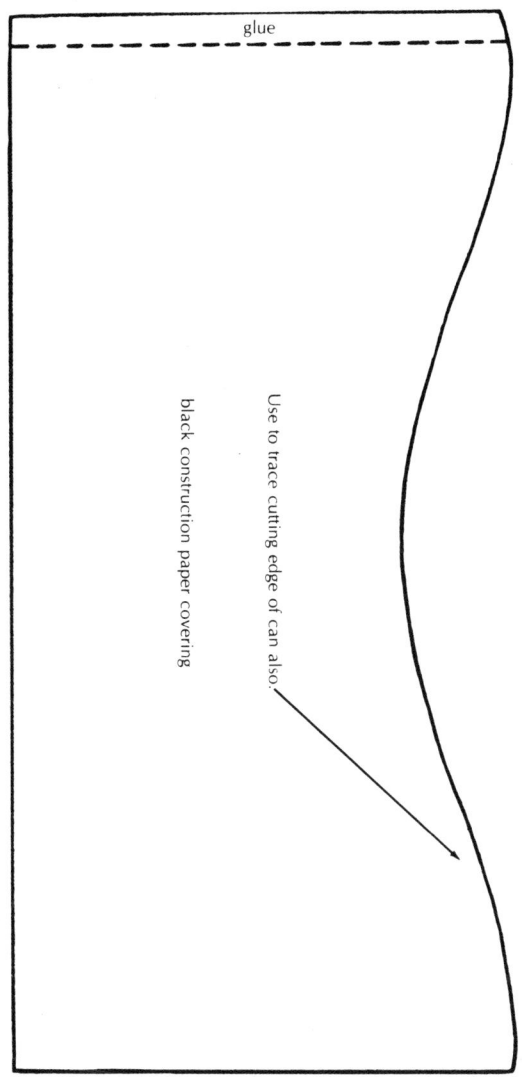

glue

black construction paper covering

Use to trace cutting edge of can also

Black construction paper (can covering)
8¾" x 4⅛"
Black construction paper circles (two)
3" diameter
Black construction paper strip 9½" x ⅛"
Light tan construction paper (face) 3¼" x 3"
Eyes made from black and white punched circles
¼" and ⅛" paper punches
Fingernail scissors (for pattern making)
Scissors
Narrow black marking pen
White glue
A tacky glue
Red crayon

*Assembly:*

Trace and cut all pieces. Cover the corrugated piece on one side (to be underneath) and glue the narrow black strip around the edge. Use the covering pattern to mark the can, which is then cut with scissors on the traced line. Spread glue on the cutout crown with your finger. Place the yellow or gold construction paper on it, then trim it to fit the cardboard crown. Overlap the crown ¼" and glue together. Glue half the hinge to the top (uncovered side) and the other half to the tallest part (back) of the can. Use a tacky glue to glue the black covering around the plastic can.

Trace the face on tan paper, making details with a marker pen, including the moustache. Color his lips with a red crayon. Glue eyes in place where indicated. When you make a pattern for the face with cutouts, you will be certain to have the eyes, nose, and mouth all in the same places on all copies. It makes tracing easier, too. Glue the other black circle to the top of the corrugated circle. Glue the face on the lowest arc of the can, along the edge. Glue the edge of the crown and set on top the black circle (lid).

King Saul wasn't very happy, so he wears a frown. This can be used to store or save any number of things, including memory verses. You can make a small name plate of white construction paper and glue it to the can covering.

# The Boy's Lunch

*Materials needed:*
6" x 7" piece of white-faced light cardboard
Ice pick
Single edge razor blade
Brown felt ¼" x 5½" (ties)
24" brown cotton rug, acrylic, or Dacron yarn
Crayons
Black narrow marking pen
White glue
Scissors
Ruler

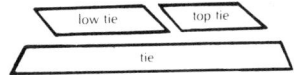

low tie     top tie

tie

two fish     five loaves

# Ten Commandments Box

**Materials needed:**

Two pieces of corrugated cardboard 4" x 3½" (for front and back)

Two pieces corrugated cardboard 3¾" x 1" (long sides)

Two pieces corrugated cardboard 2½" x 1" (short sides)

Lightweight white interfacing 2½" x 1¼" (hinge)

Electric saber saw with knife-edge blade

White glue

Gray or brown acrylic paint

¼" and smaller brushes

Black narrow marking pen

Ruler

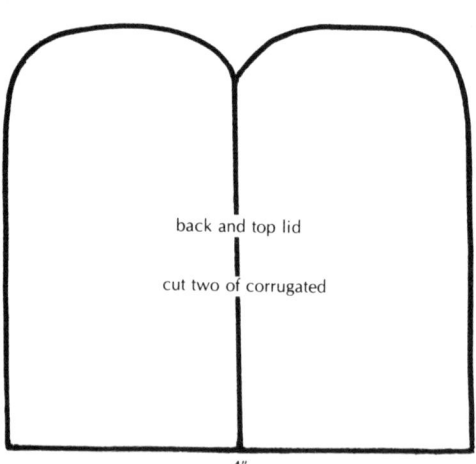

back and top lid

cut two of corrugated

4"

*Assembly:*

If you cut the bag from the pattern, it will be easy to trace the inner outline of the bag. Punch the holes in the pattern so they will all be uniform. Lay the pattern on the 6" x 7" white-faced cardboard and trace around the bag outline. Mark the punched out holes of the pattern onto the 6" x 7" cardboard. Use the ice pick to pierce the holes through. Use the razor blade in a sawing motion on the back to remove the protruding cardboard.

Put some glue on one end of the yarn and twist to form a needle (cotton, then Dacron, works best). When it is dry, it is easy for a child to sew through the holes. Glue the one end (on the back) at the starting place. Draw the needle through to the right side before giving it to a child. It will assure him of starting in the proper hole.

Trace the fish and loaves on the inside of the lunch bag. (This isn't the type bag used in the story, but the children can more readily identify it as a lunch bag.) This could be used as a money bag, too, for the story of the widow's mite, etc. by replacing the fish and loaves with coins. (Print "The Boy's Lunch" at the lower right-hand corner of the cardboard.) Let the child color the fish, loaves, lunch bag, and make grass. Cut the ties from felt before giving them to the child. Let him glue or paste them in place after he has sewn around the edges.

*Assembly:*

Remember to keep the printing on corrugated material to the inside of the box. Verses for memorization can be typed and put inside the completed box. Cut all corrugated parts with the saber saw. The shorter sidepieces fit inside the two longer ones. Glue these to form a rectangle. When they are dry enough to pick up, glue around the top edges. Turn the rectangle upside down onto the printed side of the stone bottom, keeping the edges against the left edge of the stone bottom (flush), and against the bottom edge. Only the top (curved) and the far right have margins. Set the top on the rectangle (don't glue). Keep the left and lower edges all flush. Spread glue on half the hinge area

starting hole

on the lid with your finger and the other half down the side of the box. When the glue is dry, paint the box with acrylic paint. You can leave the inside of the box paintless if desired. When the paint is thoroughly dry, use a ruler and separate the two tablets. With the black marker pen, put Roman or another kind of numerals down both left sides of the stone tablets. Make a wavy line from the numbers to indicate the Commandments.

# Boy Jesus in Temple

*Materials needed:*
  7" x 6½" white construction paper
  Two pieces 4" x 2⅛" brown construction paper
  White glue
  Black narrow marking pen
  #1724 "Story of Jesus" seal (Standard Publishing)
  Crayons
  Scissors
  Ruler

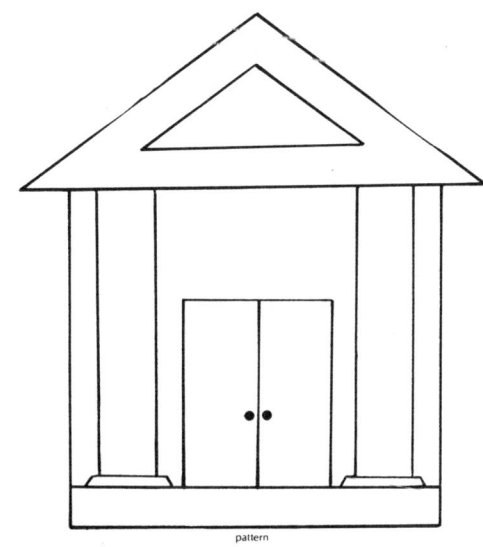

pattern

*Assembly:*
  There are two patterns to help you to trace lines easily. Trace around the largest one. From the second pattern, cut out the sections marked with X. When you trace the temple, lay one pattern on top

aid to tracing pattern

the other to trace the pillars, etc. (This greatly simplifies tracing.) Use a ruler to finish tracing the lines. Make all lines with a black marking pen and ruler after they have been traced with a pencil. (This saves your pattern.) Color all parts except the door section. Glue the cut apart doors on the outside to cover the door section. The child can open the doors of the temple and find Jesus glued inside.

# Balaam's Donkey

*Materials needed:*
  White-faced light cardboard 6½" x 7"
  ⅛" paper punch
  ⅜" paper fastener
  3/16" or ¼" moving eye (or make one of punched construction paper)
  White glue
  Black narrow marking pen
  Scissors
  Brown or gray crayon

*Assembly:*
  Trace and cut all parts from white-faced light cardboard. Notice the one pattern is only a tracing aid, not part of the donkey (included only for marking the back of the donkey, so children will know exactly where the tab will be glued). Make all markings with a black marking pen. You can leave the hoofs undone so the child can color them also. When it is colored, put the paper fastener from the

front of the donkey through the legs pattern. Turn over and glue only the tips of the tab sparingly. Place the tab over the legs pattern in the place indicated by the traced tab lines. Glue an eye in place.

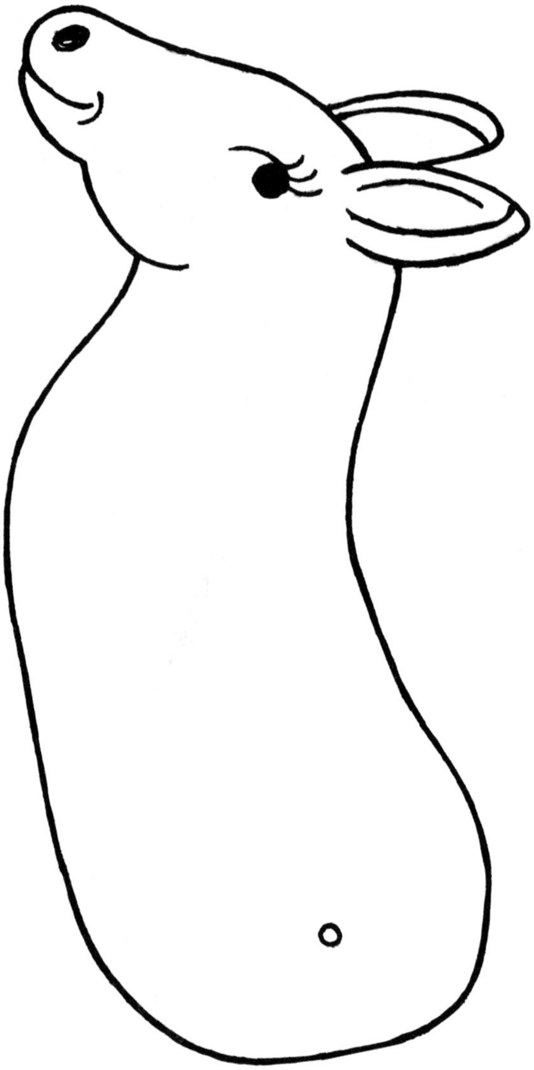

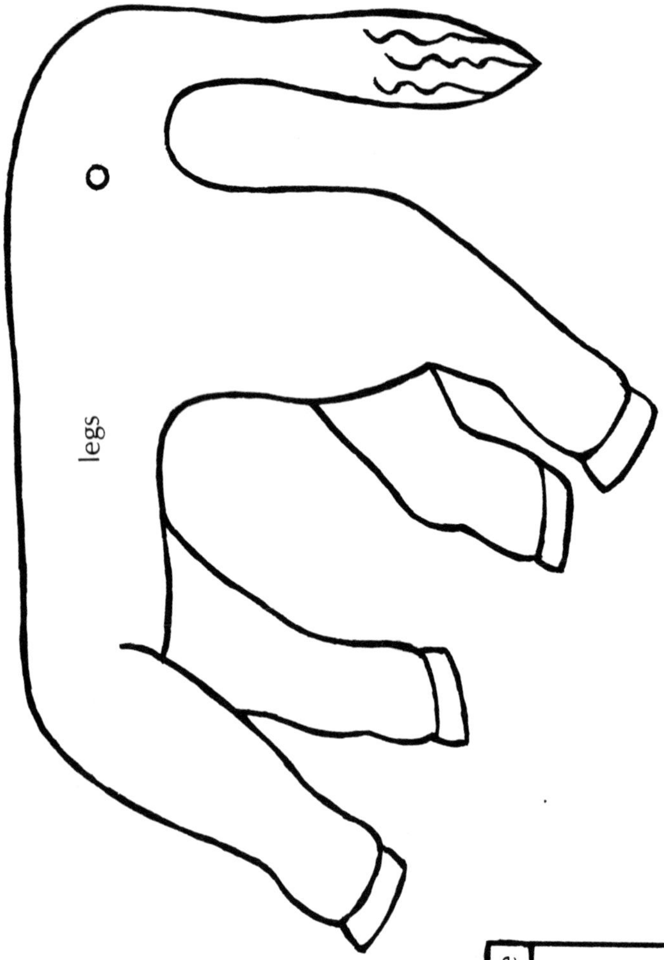

legs

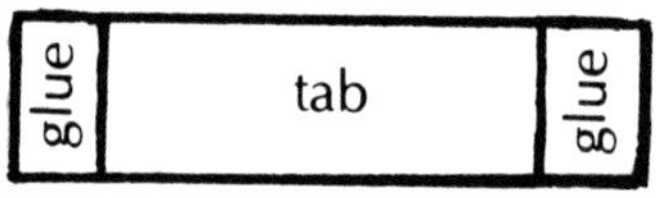

glue tab glue

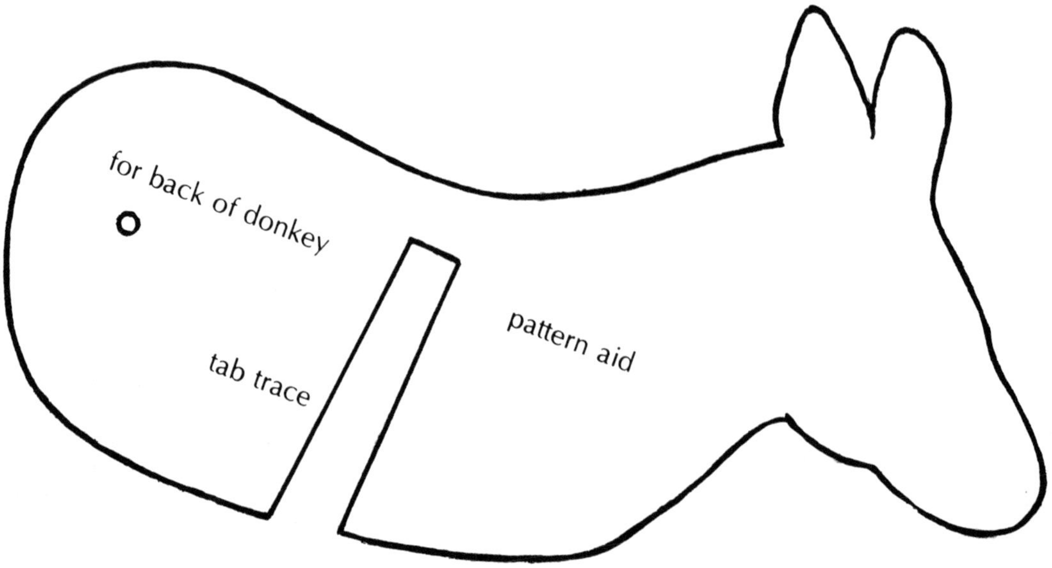

for back of donkey

tab trace

pattern aid

# Baby Jesus

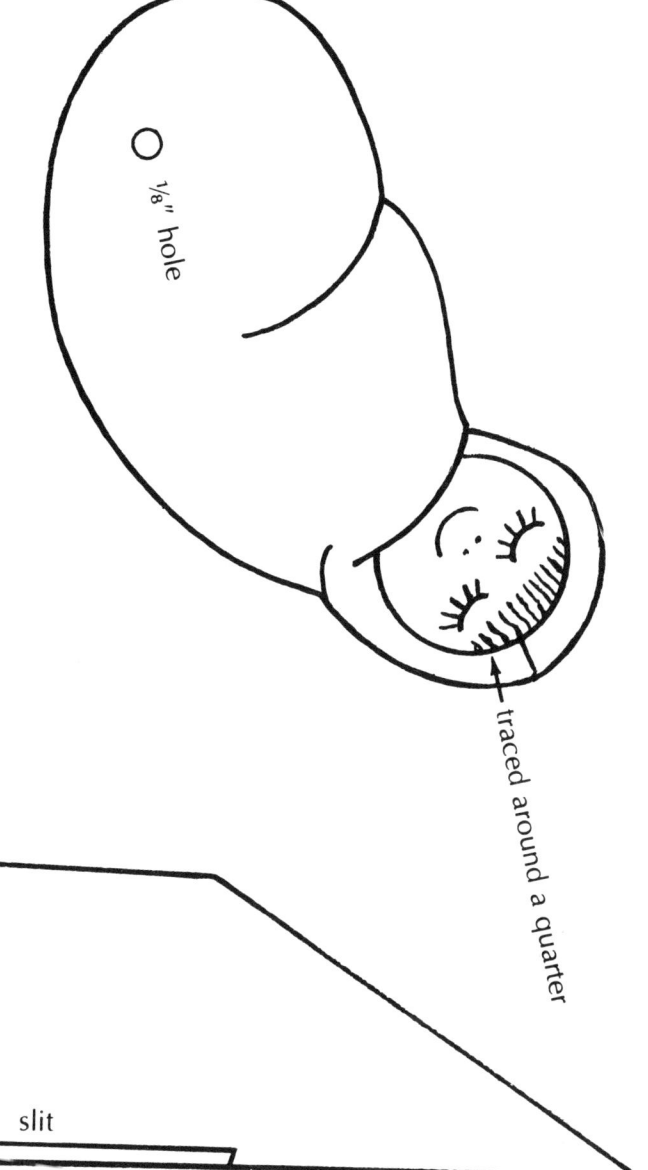

1/8" hole

traced around a quarter

*Materials needed:*
  White-faced light cardboard 7" x 5"
  Black and red narrow marker pens
  Scissors
  Crayons
  3/8" paper fastener
  1/8" paper punch
  Single edge razor blade
  White glue
  Grass in yellow or green (waxed type, but not
    cellophane)

1/8" hole O

slit

# Jonah and the Great Fish

*Assembly:*
  Trace and cut both pieces out of white cardboard. Punch hole in Jesus figure. Cut slit out with a sharp razor blade. Punch hole in manger. Make all markings with black marker pen. Color figures. Glue sparingly along the lower edge of the manger (under slit). Press cut up grass into the glue. Slip figure into the slit. Put a fastener through the manger, then through Jesus figure.

*Materials needed:*

Light white-faced cardboard (background)
9" x 4¼"
Light white-faced cardboard (Jonah and top jaw)
3" x 3"
⅜" paper fastener
Black thin-lined marker pen
Gray, black, blue, and another color (Jonah's gown) crayons
Single edge razor blade
Scissors
⅛" paper punch
Ice pick
Pencil

*Assembly:*

Trace patterns onto the cardboard and cut out Jonah and the top jaw. One large pattern is only a tracing aid. Lay it on top the background drawing to trace the division line between the light and dark gray parts of the great fish. It assures all finished products will be alike. Go over lines with black marker pen. Punch the hole on the background piece with the ice pick. Use a razor blade to saw the protruding cardboard off the back of the piece. Make an eye on the top section of the fish, a half inch behind the punch hole. Cut the slit with a sharp razor blade by laying the piece on a heavy layer of newspapers. Make wavy water with a blue crayon all around the fish, to just above the top tail.

Trace the tiny figure of Jonah onto the proper place of the top jaw. Go over the lines with the black marker pen. Color the whole fish with a gray crayon. Color the top of the fish lightly with the black crayon. Color Jonah's gown any color you like. Color the background around Jonah gray, if desired.

To assemble, slip the lower section into the fish's jaw slit, align the punched holes, and put the paper fastener in place.

(The great fish swallows Jonah and opens its mouth to cast him out.)

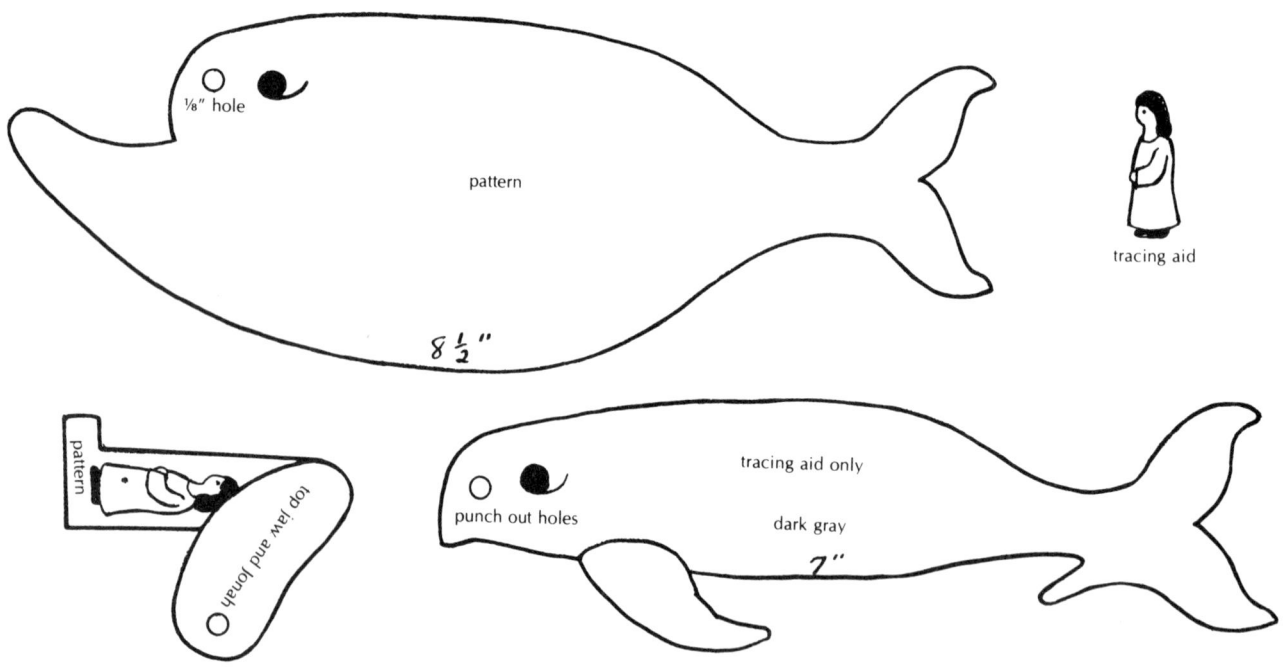

⅛" hole

pattern

tracing aid

8 ½ "

pattern

top jaw and Jonah

punch out holes

tracing aid only

dark gray

7 "

# Ascension of Jesus

*Materials needed:*

Light cardboard (white front) 8" x 6"
Single edge razor blade
Black narrow marking pen
Crayons
Scissors
#1724 "Story of Jesus" seals (Standard Publishing)
Electric saber saw with knife-edge blade (optional)
White-faced light cardboard for figures, clouds (two), and tab
Corrugated cardboard 3½" x ½"

Corrugated cardboard (two pieces) about ⅜″ square
White glue

*Assembly:*

Cut all parts from materials. You can cut the squares and longer strip from corrugate with a single edge razor blade. But if you are doing it for several children, use a saber saw for speed. Cut the Jesus seal to fit the top of the one cloud. (One pattern is only for marking the place on the back of this cloud to aid a child or yourself in gluing the tab in the proper place.) Cut the two slits over a thickness of newspaper with a single edge razor blade. Glue the tab on one side only with a very thin amount of glue. Slide the unglued tab in one (top) slot and out the other (lower slot). With your finger apply a thin amount of glue to the unglued side of the tab and press down. Color background and figures.

Glue the corrugated squares, one to the far right lower edge of the straight line of the large cloud. Glue the other square to the upper left part of the same cloud. Put another dot of glue on the squares and place the cloud so it is about ½″ down from the top of the card background. The right edge of the cloud should be even with the right edge of the background card.

Glue the corrugated strip to the lower left edge. Then glue the three figures to the top of it. Jesus ascends to Heaven, disappearing into the cloud.

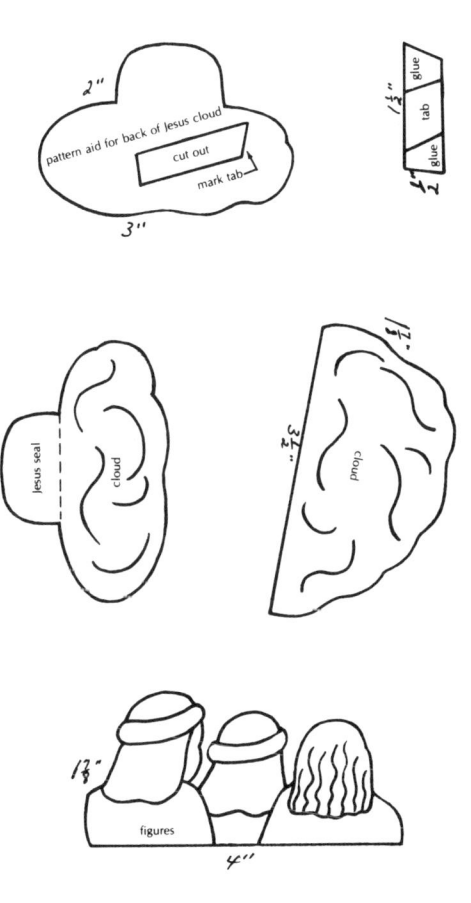

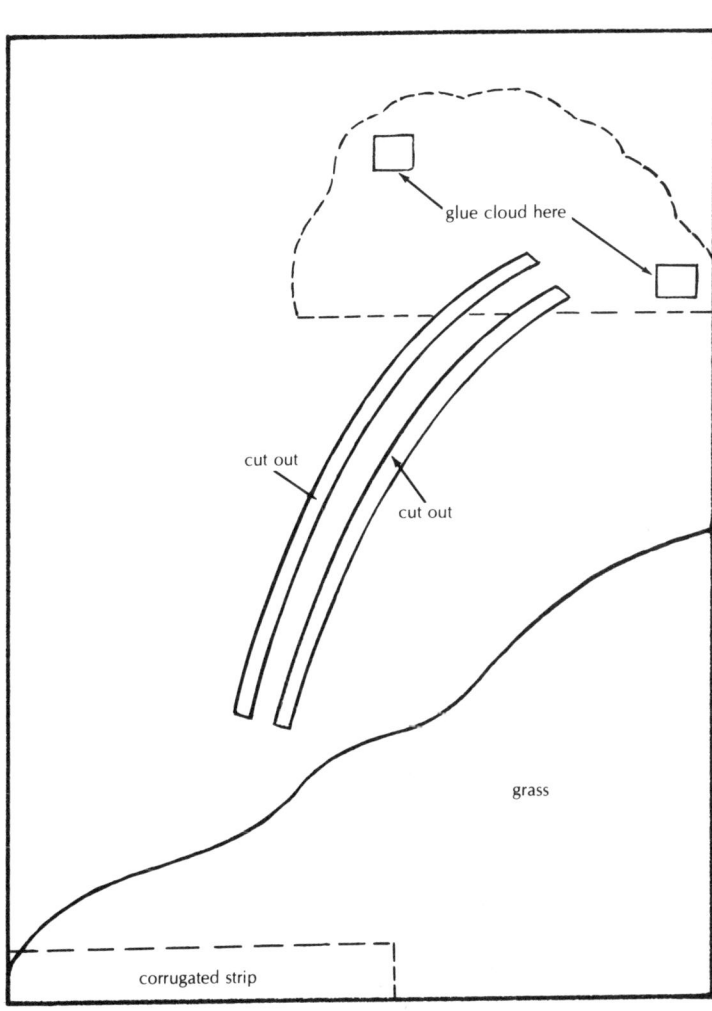

# Noah and the Rainbow

*Materials needed:*

Light white-faced cardboard 7⅜″ x 4½″
Light white cardboard 2″ x 4½″ (sky)
Four pieces light cardboard (to lift sky forward) 2″ x ¼″
Light white cardboard (rainbow)
Light cardboard (back lift)

Lightweight white interfacing (lift tab) ½″ x 2″
Crayons
Ruler
Black narrow marking pen
Scissors
White glue
Single edge razor blade

*Assembly:*

Cut all parts. You can draw Noah by cutting figure from the traced pattern picture and tracing him in place. Cut slits with a single edge razor blade over newspaper thicknesses. After the whole background cardboard has been traced, and the lines defined with the marking pen, color it. Color the sky piece the same color blue you use for the sky.

Color the rainbow in single lines (from bottom to top) with various crayons—purple, blue, green, yellow, orange, and red. Slip the tabs through each slit so the tabs are behind the picture. Turn the picture over and glue the lifting bar very thinly on each end. Press it over the rainbow tabs. Double the interfacing. Leave about ½" sticking up in the center for the child to hold. Glue the rest to the center of the lift bar. Let dry.

Glue one of the cardboard ½" strips on top of another one. Do the same with the remaining two. Now you have two pieces, joined. Glue one of these pieces to the left front top edge of the picture. Glue the other to the top right edge. Put glue on top these strips and set the sky on them.

When dry, the child can raise and lower the rainbow with the aid of the tab at the back of the picture. If it seems to bind some, bend the back of the background backwards and slightly bow the sky piece forward.

7⅜"

4½"

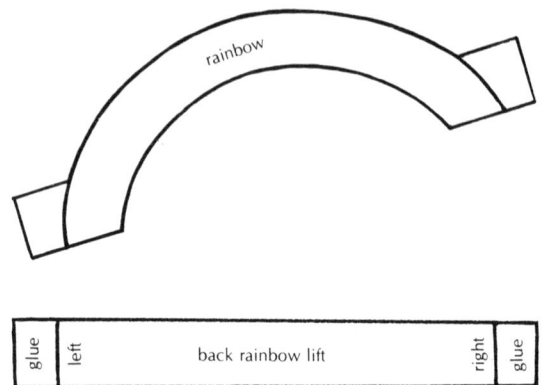

rainbow

| glue | left | back rainbow lift | right | glue |

# FAVORS AND CENTERPIECES

## Patriotic Favor

*Materials needed:*
   Red construction paper (hat)
   White construction paper (notes of music)
   Blue construction paper (arms and base)
   Flesh color construction paper (brown, pink, yellow, etc.)
   Red and white striped gift wrap (usually available at Christmas)
   1½" square of corrugated cardboard (base)
   Light cardboard (for patterns)
   Blue plastic ice cream stick
   White plastic creamer container
   2" piece of a small size plastic straw
   Very tiny piece of a blue feather
   Single edge razor blade
   Rubber cement
   White glue
   Hot melt glue
   Tuna type can
   Toothpicks
   Scissors
   Black marking pen (narrow)
   Hand iron (electric) for pressing one end of plastic straw
   Gold spray paint
   Black enamel (for model airplanes)
   Small bristle brush
   Brown grocery sack (for pressing straw)
   Electric saber saw with knife-edge blade

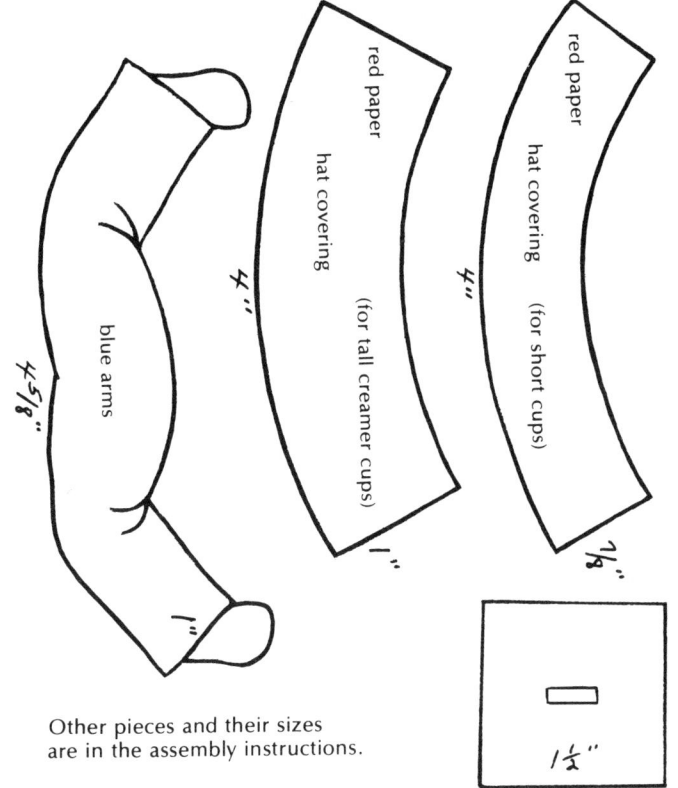

Other pieces and their sizes are in the assembly instructions.

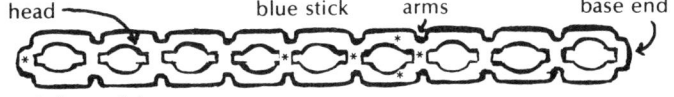

head — blue stick   arms   base end

*glue points

*Assembly:*

See the directions in this book on "Mr. and Mrs. Rabbit" for cutting a feather to get small feathers for the hat.

Trace all patterns and cut from whatever paper is indicated. Glue the flesh hands (same color you use for the face) onto the blue arms. Glue the one featured head to the plain flesh head. (Features are done with a narrow marking pen, or, if flesh is brown or black, use a light-colored drawing pencil.) Glue red construction paper around the creamer hat, gluing at seam. (Seams are always to the back of the figure.) Glue a striped strip of red and white gift wrap (⅛" x 4½") close to the brim of the hat. Trace music bars and notes on white construction paper with a black marking pen. Cut it out, leaving the bar and marks at top and bottom showing. (Cut carefully.)

Place a piece of grocery sack over a third of the plastic straw and lightly press it. You don't want to melt it, only squeeze it some. Put these flutes on a chenille wire, stuck into an egg carton, and spray them with gold paint. When they are dry, use a toothpick to put dots on the flat side and to the end of the flute, about ¼" apart. There should be five black dots (flute holes.) Allow to dry thoroughly.

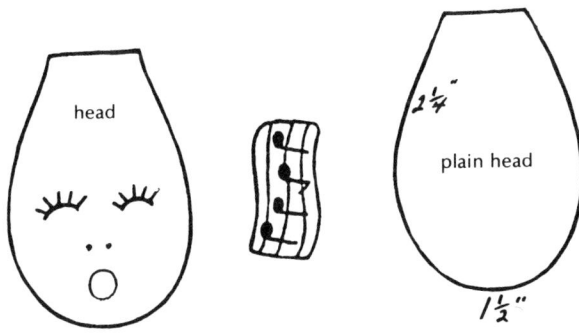

head

plain head

2¼"

1½"

Cut the corrugated square with an electric saber saw, or you can do it with a single edge razor blade. Coat the top of the square (printed side, if the corrugated cardboard has print on it) with rubber cement. Coat the square of red and white striped gift wrap with rubber cement, too. Do the same with a ¼" x 6¾" blue strip for the edges of the corrugated square. Let all dry, then very carefully put the square of red and white striped paper over the corrugated square. (Do it very carefully, and it sticks very well.) Put the blue strip around the exposed edges of the corrugated square the same way. If this proves too difficult, you can use your finger and spread white glue (thinly) over the corrugated square and put the striped gift wrap on. It must be very thinly spread, or the red and white paper will wrinkle. Use the square pattern to mark the slit in the striped corrugated cardboard base. Cut it out with a razor blade. You want to go through all the cardboard except the very bottom layer. Remove the cut out slice.

With a dot of white glue, put the tiny feather on the right side of the hat (as you look at it) above the striped hatband. Feather is to your right, and the hat seam is to the back.

Melt hot melt glue in the tin can (shallow one) over a low heat, so it doesn't scorch and become brown in color. Use the toothpick to put glue on, when indicated in instructions. Touch the plastic stick to the hot glue and immediately place it in the slit of the corrugated square. (Is it standing straight?) The glue dries rapidly. The top four sections of the blue plastic stick will be glued behind the head, so put a dot of hot glue at the top of the stick and at the top of the fourth section. Immediately stick the face to the plastic stick so the top of the head is no higher than the top of the plastic stick.

Now you will place the hat on the head. The hat will tilt to the back, so the eyes can be seen. Pick up the stick (base attached). Touch it into the hot glue and immediately to the very inside top, as closely to the front as possible. The back of the hat is pressed toward you, until the sides of the face just touch the sides of the hat.

Down half a section from where the head ends, begin to put hot glue dots on the back of the stick (half a section and the next section). Place the arm piece onto the hot glue. You can see the hands as you do this gluing. They will seem to be backwards, but, remember, the hands will come around to the front, hands upwards.

The squeezed end of the flute should be ⅛" to the right of the mouth. Go directly across the mouth so the rounded end is sticking out beyond the head. With a toothpick, put a couple dots of hot glue on the mouth near the edge of the face. Quickly press the flute to the face in a straight line.

Between the black second and third dots (squeezed end), put a dot of hot glue and set the rounded corner of the music into it so the music is going upwards, about ⅛" below the brim of the hat.

Bend the arm to your right forward. Place the hand to the flute just past the first dot of black on the flute. Crease the arm, so the hand will stay where it belongs. Put a dot of hot glue under the hand and press it to the flute. Do the left hand the same way, so that it is about where the fourth black dot is.

# Cradle Favor

*Materials needed:*
 Light cardboard
 Woodtone wallpaper
 White glue
 Small animal cutouts from catalogs
 Single edge razor blade
 Scissors

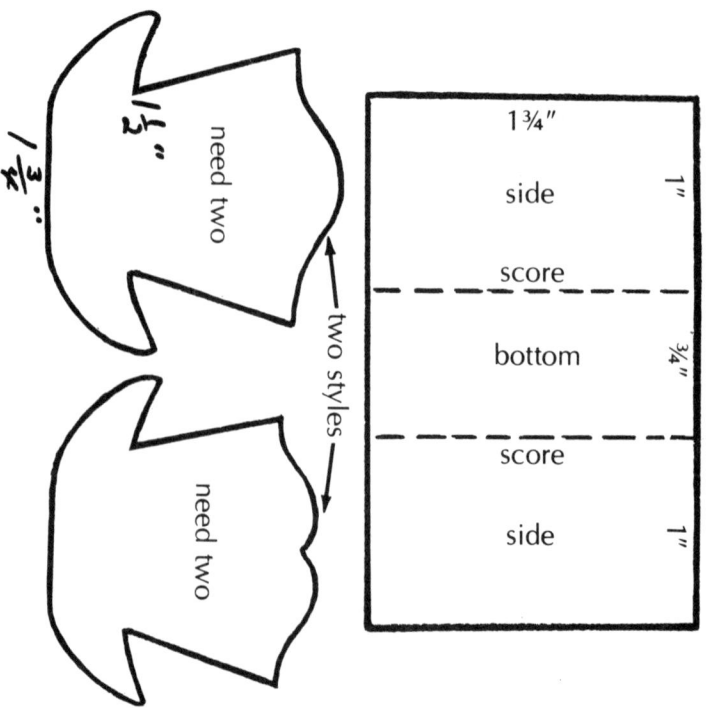

## Assembly:

Trace all pieces on light cardboard and cut them out. Score all lines lightly with the razor blade and fold all back (one way). Punch a hole where indicated on the top of the holder. Glue all tabs on the largest part and assemble it. Glue the two tabs of the front panel. Put it in place with tabs inside the sidepieces of the main body of the holder, even with the top of both sides. Glue the back of the tiny match holder piece after it's assembled. Place it in the center of the front of the holder. When dry, hand paint with poster paints or spray paint several at a time. Glue or paint a design to the tiny match holder as desired. Fill the favor from the top with tiny mints.

# Matchbox Holder Favor

Materials needed:
   5½" x 6" white light cardboard
   ⅛" paper punch
   White glue
   Scissors
   Single edge razor blade
   Poster paints or spray paint

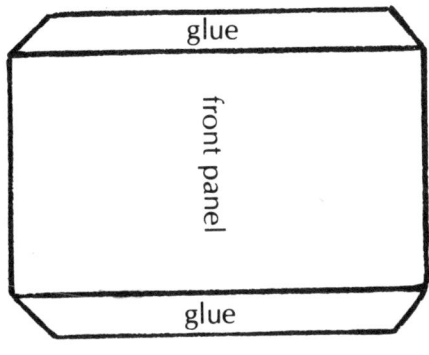

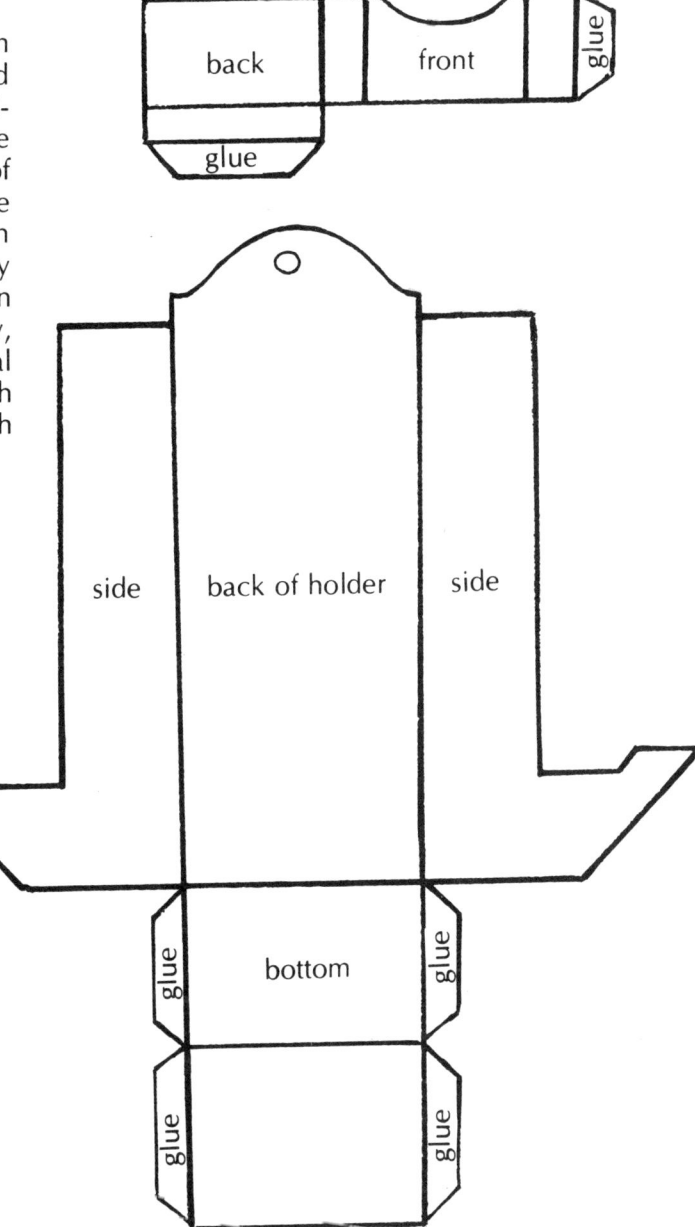

## Assembly:

Cut all pieces from light cardboard. Cut matching pieces from woodtone wallpaper and glue on other pieces. You can glue the wallpaper to the cardboad, then trim around the pieces. Watch the grain of the wallpaper for a nice looking cradle. (Use a cardboard box that is brown inside, and you need not cover both sides of the pieces.) Score the fold lines of the bottom sidepiece lightly with a razor blade. Fold along scored lines. Glue one edge of the bottom sidepiece and set it on one of the ends. Keep it close to the side of the end piece. When it holds alone, glue the other the same way. Don't overglue or it won't dry quickly. Cut a tiny design and glue one to each outside cradle end. Fill with mints, etc. This favor is a great conversation piece at baby showers.

# Bassinet Favors

*Materials needed:*

Corrugated cardboard (bottoms) 2½" x 1⅜"
Electric saber saw with knife-edge blade
Plastic white creamer cups (optional)
White construction paper to cover the corrugated bottoms
Two pieces white cardboard or construction paper (optional handles) 3¼" x ¼"
White light cardboard (sides) 7" x 1"
Felt trim 7¼" x ¼"
White construction paper bows ¾" x 2"
Acrylic paint
Plier-type stapler
White glue
Black narrow marking pen
Small brush
¼" brush
Scissors

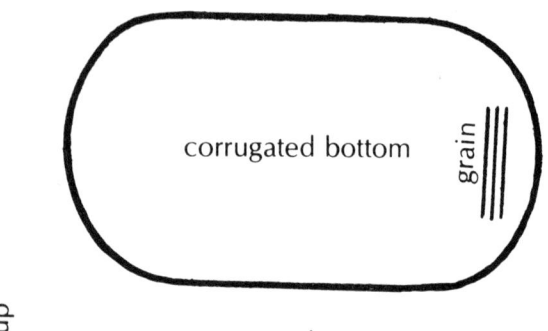

corrugated bottom

grain

cup

two bows

don't cut off square

*Assembly:*

There are three types you can make, depending on the type creamer cups you get. One favor is without a hood (has handles).

Cut the corrugated bases with the saber saw. Glue white construction paper to one or both sides of the base. Hold the side cardboard between the forefinger and thumb of your left hand and pull the piece downward, to give it curve. Glue along one long edge and across one short end. Wrap it around the base (bottom) of the bassinet, holding the overlapped seam until it will hold alone. (Use

glue sparingly on this seam. Spread with a finger.)

If you opt to put handles on, glue them in position along the outside of the bassinet, so they are even and swing outwards.

If you opt to use a creamer-cup hood, cut a section from the hood ¾" wide, but don't cut any of the bottom off. When you come to the bottom, cut around it, so the whole bottom is left intact. A single edge razor blade works well for this. You can elect to snip off the rim of the cup or leave it on (makes no difference).

Put the hood onto the bassinet so the curved creamer bottom is on the outside of the back and the sides of the cup. It should be straight. Tip the ends down slightly and staple both sides of the hood to the sides of the bassinet.

Paint it inside and out. When dry, glue the felt around the top edge of the bassinet side (seam in the back). If desired, you can also put a felt trim around the hood. Trace the bows onto white construction paper and make details with a black marker pen. Cut them out and glue one to each side with a dot of glue on the felt.

If there are any gaps between the bottom piece and the sides, they can be filled with white glue before painting. Paint will easily go over dry white glue. Fill with mints, etc.

# Swan Favor

*Materials needed:*

Electric saber saw with knife-edge blade
Corrugated cardboard 1½" x 1½" (bottom)
Corrugated cardboards 1½" x 1¼" (two sides or ends)
4" x 4" light cardboard (white on both sides)
4¾" white, yellow, black, or orange chenille wire (neck and head)
Two 1½" long feathers (cut off quill section)
Small piece of same color construction paper as head
Black and white eyes
White construction paper (covering for inside and out) 9" x 1½"
White glue
Ice pick

40

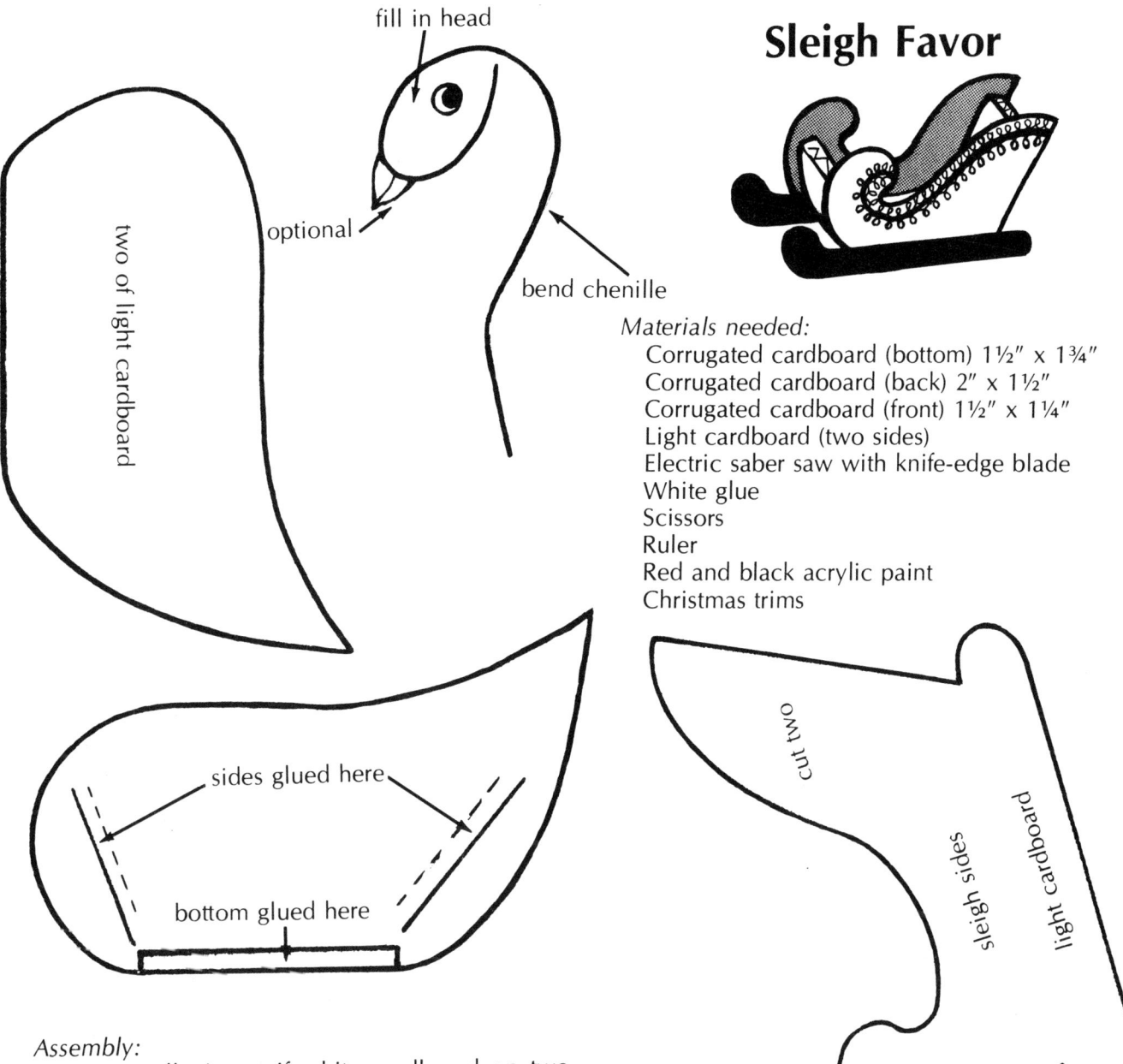

fill in head

optional

bend chenille

two of light cardboard

# Sleigh Favor

*Materials needed:*
    Corrugated cardboard (bottom) 1½" x 1¾"
    Corrugated cardboard (back) 2" x 1½"
    Corrugated cardboard (front) 1½" x 1¼"
    Light cardboard (two sides)
    Electric saber saw with knife-edge blade
    White glue
    Scissors
    Ruler
    Red and black acrylic paint
    Christmas trims

sides glued here

bottom glued here

cut two

sleigh sides

light cardboard

*Assembly:*
Cut out all pieces. If white cardboard on two sides is difficult to find, you can paint the two sides with white acrylic paint, or whatever color you desire. If used as a favor for a baby shower, you might want to make some blue and some pink.

Glue the bottom and the two ends as illustrated. Bend the chenille wire as shown. Lay it on construction paper. With a pencil trace close to the wire on the inside of the head. Cut it out and lightly run glue all around the inside of the chenille head. Press the construction piece in place so it's even. Glue the eyes in place on both sides of the paper head. Cover the inside corrugated pieces with white so the seam will be at the bottom, back (inconspicuous place). Put a dot of glue on both sides of the body and press the feathers in place so they tilt downward in the back. Ice pick the center of the front corrugated piece. Put a dot of glue on the neck and push it in the hole. Put a bill of construction paper on if desired. Fill with mints, etc.

*Assembly:*
Cut light cardboard pieces with scissors. Cut the corrugated pieces with an electric saber saw. Glue the bottom between the two sidepieces. Glue the back so it butts up against the bottom on one edge. Do the front the same way. Both front and back pieces are glued on an angle. Fill with glue any gaps between the corrugated cardboard, the light cardboard sides, and the spaces between the joints where the corrugated cardboard pieces meet. Let dry. Paint the sides red and the runners black. The inside and all else is painted red. When the paint has dried, glue Christmas trims around the side edges of the sleigh. Decorate as desired.

# Cradle Centerpiece

## Materials needed:

Electric saber saw with knife-edge blade

Corrugated cardboard for two sides, end, two rockers, 1 cradle front (top piece)

Corrugated cardboard (cradle hood top) 4" x 3½"

Corrugated cardboard (back end piece) 5⅞" x 3¼"

Corrugated cardboard (bottom) 8½" x 4"

Woodtone wallpaper

White glue

Rubber bands

Red construction paper (hearts)

Green construction paper (leaves)

## Assembly:

Cut all pieces from corrugated cardboard. Cover the exposed (curved) edges of the two rockers with woodtone wallpaper strips. Cover the rockers and bottom of the cradle on both sides. Spread white glue with your finger for better and thinner spreading. Center and glue the flat sides of the rocker edges (uncovered) back from the ends about ¾" to 1". Let dry upside down. Glue the cradle ends inside the two sidepieces after they have been covered on both sides with wallpaper. Cover the hood top and the front small piece with wallpaper. Set the small piece between the two sides, keeping all edges aligned. Glue all around the top edges of the hood and set it on with an overlap around. Remove, add more glue to the glue lines on the top, and reset. Let dry.

When the bottom with the rockers is dry, turn it right side up. Glue around the whole bottom edge of the cradle and set it on top the bottom so there is an overhang on all four sides. Remove and glue on the glue lines of the bottom and reset. Let dry. Glue strips of wallpaper on all exposed edges.

Glue the hearts and leaves on all four sides, one heart and four leaves as though it were a skull and cross sign, or any way you like.

This centerpiece can hold a small vase with flowers in it, artificial flowers, a doll for a baby shower, etc. Goes nicely with the cradle favor.

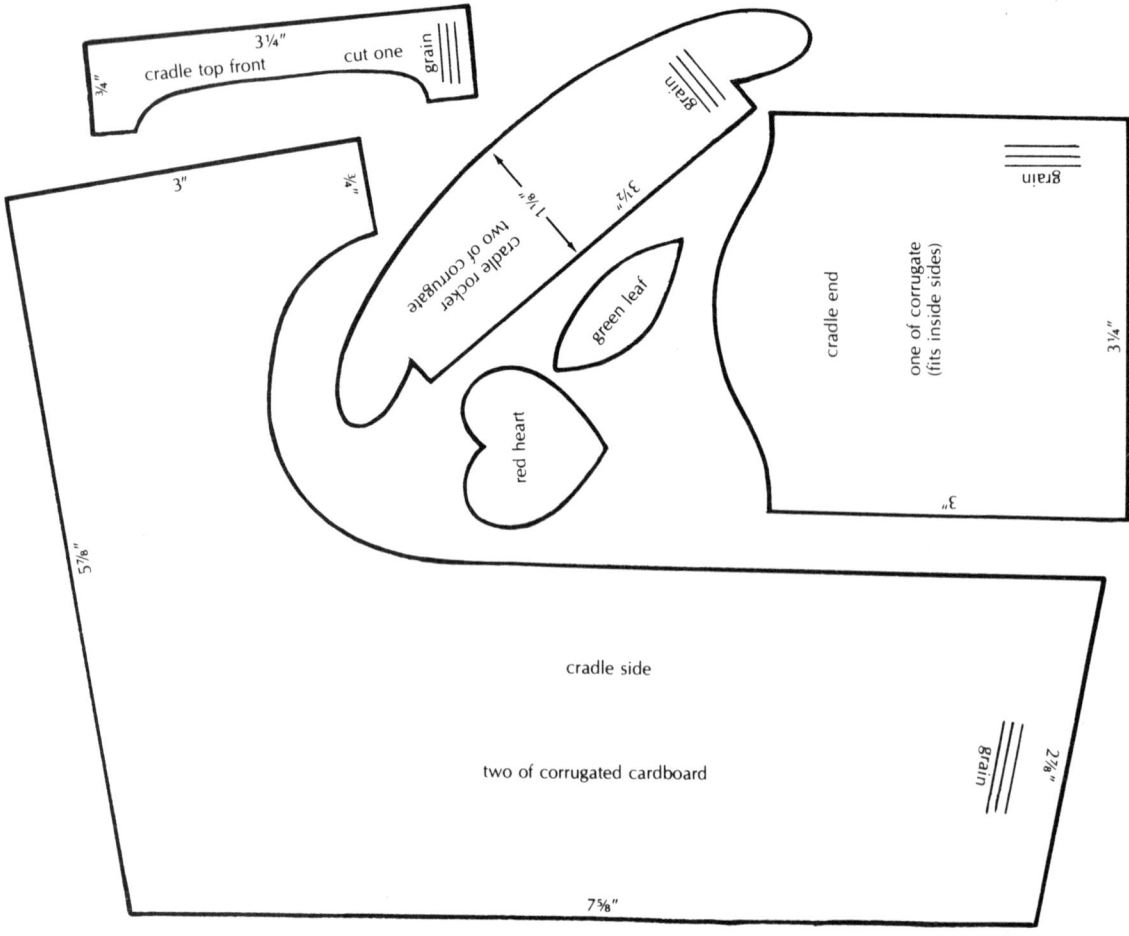

3¼"

cradle top front    cut one

grain

¾"

3"

¾"

grain

1⅛"

cradle rocker
two of corrugate

3½"

green leaf

red heart

grain

cradle end

one of corrugate
(fits inside sides)

3¼"

3"

5⅞"

cradle side

two of corrugated cardboard

grain    2⅞"

7⅝"

# Christmas Centerpiece

**Materials needed:**

  6″ diameter plastic holly stem (with red berries)
  9″ x 4½″ corrugated cardboard
  Foil gift wrap in two complimentary colors
  Cotton batting (collars and snow)
  Black acrylic rug yarn
  Red and black narrow marking pens
  Small amount of red felt
  Two plastic creamer cups 1″ tall
  7″ x 12″ light cardboard
  Two 7 oz. plastic cup liners
  Two 5″ pieces black chenille wire
  Two molded foam 1½″ diameter balls
  Acrylic paint for faces (brown, yellow flesh, etc.)
  White tacky glue
  White glue
  Electric saber saw with knife-edge blade
  Scissors
  Single edge razor blade
  Stapler
  ½″ wide brush
  Toothpicks
  Wide black marker
  Strip of woodtone wallpaper ⅛″ x 23″
  Small piece of white-faced light cardboard
    2″ x 3″
  Rubber cement

8¼″

3″

body foil coverings
plastic cup

hat crown
foil coverings

2¼″

hat brim

bend downwards

arms

arms

1¼″

2½″

songbook

1¼″

1¾″

4½″

glue figure here

cut one of corrugate

face

hole

base

face

glue figure here

9″

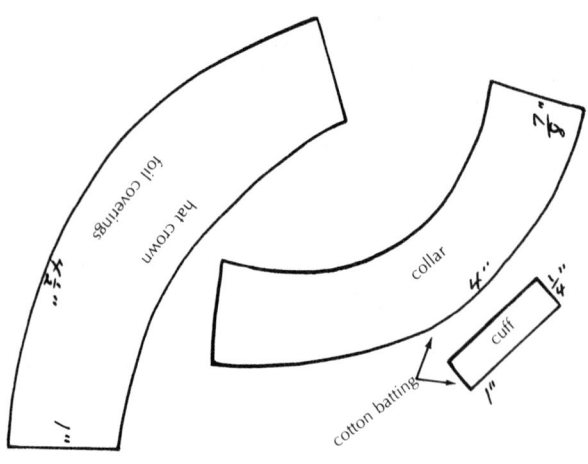

## Assembly:

Cut corrugated cardboard with saber saw. It can be cut with a razor blade also. Trace and cut all light cardboard pieces. Cut up the side of the plastic cup liners. With a sharp razor blade, cut off the top (bottom of liner). Draw the sides together, overlap until the diameter measures 3" at the wide end. Staple at both ends, near edges (insides won't matter). These liners are bodies. Creamer cups are hat crowns. Cut creamer cup edges off (looking on inside of cups) so they measure only ¾" from the cup bottom to the cut edge. Cut holly stem, leaving ½" to glue in base. Glue woodtone wallpaper strip around exposed edge of base.

In covering the hat, arms, and body with foil, use rubber cement. Coat both parts to be joined with rubber cement, allow to dry, then join. Hat and arm parts are joined to foil on one side, then excess foil is trimmed off. Turn over and repeat the process. Do not cover the hands. They are painted on one side (in pairs) with the wide black marker pen. The hat top (with tabs) is glued in place first, then the crown side is glued in place. Keep all seams to the back of the figures. Songbooks are covered on one side only, leaving the white to face the figure (inside of books). Score the foil side lightly and fold a little. Arms are curved around your fingers so they have a natural curve. The center of the hat brim is curved downwards.

Paint half the molded balls in face colors desired. You can set them atop the bodies to dry thoroughly. Cut out felts. Cut black acrylic yarn over a piece of paper, ⅛" to ¼" pieces (hair).

Set bodies onto the base with tacky glue around edges of wide bottoms. Gouge center hole in the corrugated base, leaving the bottom layer of base intact. Spread white glue all over top of base, but not in hole. Press bits of cotton into glue. Fill gouge with tacky glue and set the holly stem into the hole. Cut collars from batting. You can cut cuffs, too, if desired. Glue collars onto the edges of the neck on the bodies. Glue opposite arms onto bodies below (¼") the collar. There should be a gap of 1¼" between the arms on the back of the figures.

Put tacky glue on the neck edge of the body and set head into it, so faces are in opposite directions, as the arms are. Glue creamer cups to the back of the heads with tacky glue, ¼" above the collar. Glue felt mouth to the face, just above the collar. Make two nostrils above the mouth with red marker. On dark skinned figures, you may wish to apply red enamel with a toothpick. Make eyes with a black marker as illustrated. With tacky glue around the crown, carefully wrap the brim close to it. There is a gap behind the crown where the brim doesn't meet. Form the chenille wire into a circle with ½" overlap. Glue around the brim, where it meets the crown, with tacky glue and carefully press the chenille wire into it with the overlap to the back.

Spread tacky glue, with the aid of a toothpick, to areas in front of the hat brim and down the face to the back of the hat. With a pinch of hair, press it into the glue. When all hair (yarn) is applied, tap off the excess. In skipped areas, apply more glue and repeat the process.

These are nice for banquet tables. They can be awarded as prizes by placing random numbers in the programs which correspond to the number of centerpieces you have.

# HOLIDAY CRAFTS

## Shamrock Pin

**Materials needed:**

One 12" green tinsel (plain) or green chenille wire

Green construction paper strip 8" x ¾"

Green construction paper circles 1⅛" diameter and ¾" diameter

⅛" punch

Pin for back ½" long (old torch pins)

Wide marker (used as a bending tool)

White construction paper ⅛" x 2¾" (hat band)

Very tiny feather 1" x ⅜" wide (feathers can be cut to size)

Pencil

Scissors

Hot melt glue in tuna can

A tacky glue

Light cardboard circle ¾" diameter

Toothpick

\* press together at these points

shamrock bending

inside of wire (11")

hat brim — punch hole

1" wire

bend for hat

**Assembly:**

Cut the tinsel or chenille wire into pieces measuring 11" and 1". Trace around a penny for the ¾" diameter circles. Trace all circles, plus a circle of green construction paper to glue over the cardboard circle. Punch a hole in the large 1⅛" diameter circle, as indicated. Use the marker as a bending tool, just below the cap where there is a natural groove. Bend the 11" wire around the groove so it goes just a little beyond. Remove it and bend the rest of the wire sharply back (you've made one petal or leaf of the shamrock). Wind the wire around the groove the same way to form the second leaf, using your thumbnail to hold the wire in the groove as you bend the rest with your left hand. Do the third leaf the same way, ending with the sharp bending. You have a piece left to wrap around the barrel of the marker to form the shamrock stem.

The circle with the hole punched in it is the hat brim. The other circle is the hat top. The circle glued to the cardboard is for the pin. First glue the circle with hot melt glue to the center of the green side. The back of this circle will receive hot melt glue for the pin to be pushed into.

To attach the shamrock to the green circle of cardboard, melt the glue over a low heat until it is in a liquid state. (It strings, so work with a toothpick and a twisting motion as you transfer the glue to the green side of the cardboard circle.) Put hot glue on top the green side, as it lays on a flat surface. By pressing between the shamrock leaves (illustrated), you can form the shamrock as you lay it into the glued circle. Blow on it if the glue doesn't dry fast enough to hold it together. It will dry very quickly, however. Bend the 1" wire as illustrated. With a toothpick, put a dot of hot melt glue in the center of the shamrock and set the tiny bend into it.

Glue the pin to the back of the cardboard circle with a toothpick and hot melt glue. If you have access to the small plastic torch pins, cut the base off with scissors, wire cutters, or snips so it won't stick below the circle.

Form the hat by wrapping the green strip of paper around the barrel of an object that measures ⅝" diameter. Glue the end of the strip of paper to form the side of the hat. Glue the feather and stick it at an angle to the side of the hat. A tiny dot of glue on one end of the feather is enough. Give the white band a curve around your finger by pulling it. Glue the band to the hat by using a tiny dot of glue in three places. Keep all seams to the back of the hat. Glue around the edge of the hatband and center it on the large circle so the hole in the circle is toward the front of the hat and the feather curves to the back. Glue around the edge of the hat on top and immediately place the circle of green on. When it is dry, put a large dot of white glue on the one inch stem. Set the hat on the stem so the glue will touch the inside of the hat. These make nice little gifts for children, shut-ins, etc.

# Angel Ornament

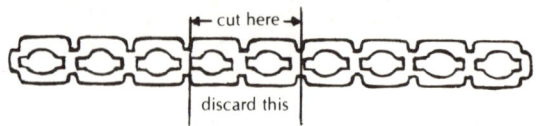

**Materials needed:**

- Two plastic ice cream sticks (yellow, and have holes in them)
- Felt 6" x 3" (your choice of color)
- ¾" diameter wooden bead
- 6" of green string
- Two pieces of tiny Christmas garland trim (silver or gold) 2" and 5½"
- Light cardboard 6" x 3" or pulp egg carton
- Corrugated cardboard ⅜" square
- Hot melt glue
- Tuna (shallow) tin
- Toothpick
- Dampened sponge
- Single edge razor blade
- White glue
- Scissors

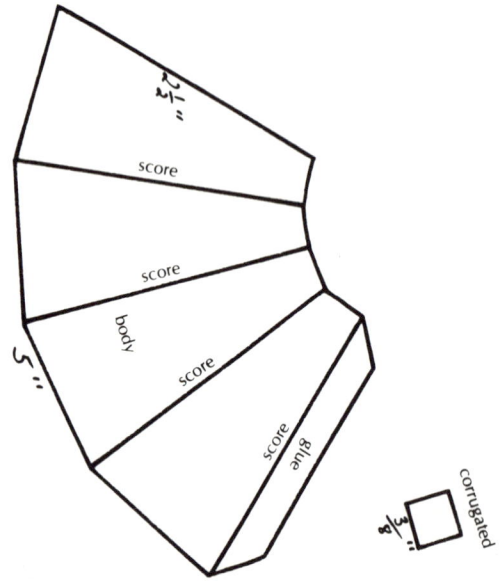

*Assembly:*

These angels are easily made from pulp egg cartons with tall peaks, if you can find the cartons. If you have no egg cartons, cut the body from light cardboard. Use the same pattern for the felt covering, but make it a little wider to go around the body cardboard. Cut the square of corrugated cardboard and the gold or silver garland (used to tie Christmas gifts). Cut the piece of green string. Cut the plastic ice cream stick as shown in the diagram. When you have everything cut, put the hot melt glue in the tuna can over a low heat. It must be melted to a thin glue. (This glue will brown if you put it on too much heat, but it won't harm its use.) With this hot melt glue, you need the toothpick for application.

As the glue heats, begin to construct the angel's body. Glue the tab to the inside of the body. (You have scored all fold lines lightly with the razor blade for neat folding.) Glue around the square of corrugated cardboard and slip it inside the body from the large open end. Rest it squarely with the top of the body. Let it dry. Glue the felt covering around the angel's body, allowing the seam to be in the center of one of the flat sides. This will be the back of the angel.

Now you will do all your gluing with hot melt glue. The wooden bead head is touched into the hot melt glue. The very front of the body (opposite the felt seam) is where the face of the angel should be. Behind the head, about ½" down from the top of the angel's body, is where you will glue the wings. With the toothpick, coat both sides (flat sides) of the section that has four holes (always on the part that's been cut with your scissors, so the wing tops are neat). Put it on the back of the angel. The other four holed piece of plastic stick butts up against the one you just put on, so the tops of the wings are about ⅛" from the head. Now do the same with the two shorter wings, but these are glued on top the longer parts that are already in place.

Again, with the toothpick, touch into the hot glue and put a dot behind the angel's head. Touch your finger to the wet sponge and press the shorter garland into the glue. Put a spot on the angel's forehead and do the same. Finish with it beside the back end. The garland around the base of the gown is done in the same manner, starting at the center felt seam, dotting the corners and centers of each section. Fold the green string in half. Put a dot of glue in the bead hole. With your damp finger, push the string ends firmly to the bead. Beautiful as a gift for a tree.

# Nativity Dome

**Materials needed:**

Corrugated cardboard (floor) 1½″ x ¾″
Corrugated cardboard (back) 4½″ x 1½″
Electric saber saw with knife-edge blade
Light cardboard (white on one side for walls)
   1⅝″ x 10¹⁵/₁₆″
Light cardboard (lamb) 2″ x 1¼″
Black narrow marking pen
Picture of nativity from card or bulletin (cut to fit
   back)
Waxed type Easter straw in green or yellow
White glue
Scissors
Ruler
Acrylic paint (outside wall, back, and front floor)
Single edge razor blade
¼″ brush

*Assembly:*

Cut all pieces from materials listed. Make details on lamb with black marker pen. Glue picture to one side of corrugated cardboard (printed side, if it has printing on it). Glue floor piece to front of picture at the very bottom. Glue around one long length and the two shorter lengths of the wall piece on the white side. (The scored line in the center of this piece is on the opposite side.) Start at the bottom and keep the edges flush with the corrugated edges. Glue the holes of the front corrugation closed. Spread a thin layer of glue on the floor with your finger. Press Easter grass onto the glue. When all is dry, paint the front edge of the floor, sides, and back. Painting the underside is optional. Glue the lamb when the floor paint is dry. (Glue just his three legs.) Put him in place to the far right. His back leg is free beyond the wall.

# Christmas Decoration

**Materials needed:**

Corrugated cardboard 8″ x 3½″
Red construction paper 3″ x 2″
White construction paper 4″ x 2″
Four pieces of 2″ green chenille bumps
Two molded foam 1″ balls
Two pulp type egg carton peaks
Artificial grass to cover corrugated base (used in
   model trains)
Four construction paper eyes
Acrylic paint in green, brown, and flesh
Black and red narrow marking pens
Brushes
White glue
Ice pick
⅛″ and ³/₁₆″ paper punches (eyes)
Toothpick
Long-nose pliers with wire cutter on them

*Assembly:*

Cut the egg carton peaks as tall as possible. Paint them green. Paint the balls flesh color (half of each ball). Cut chenille bumps apart.

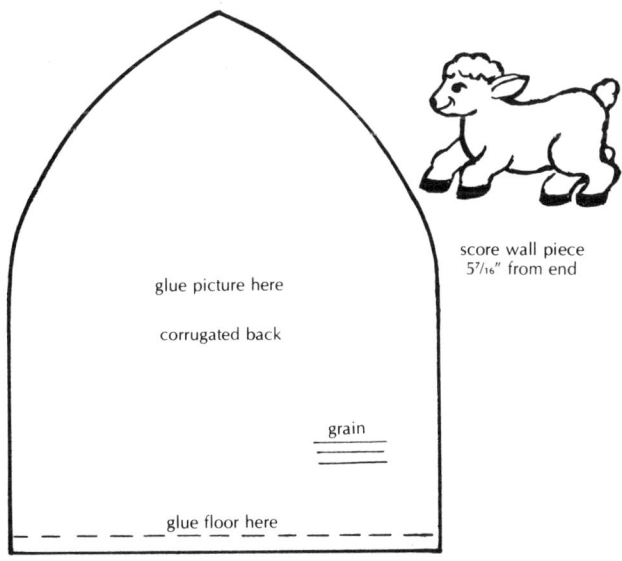

glue picture here

corrugated back

grain

glue floor here

score wall piece
5⁷/₁₆″ from end

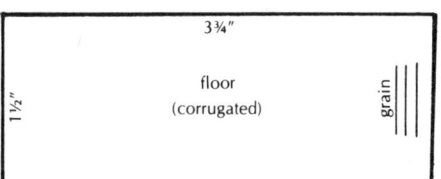

3¾″

floor
(corrugated)

1½″

grain

arm bend

mitten

hat brim

base

front

head

MERRY CHRISTMAS

Cut the corrugated base with an electric saber saw. Cut artificial grass to fit the top of this base, and a narrow strip 20″ long to go around the edge. Glue both to the base, spreading glue with your finger. Trim as needed.

Trace and cut a white construction paper banner. On it print "Merry Christmas" with a red marking pen. Trace and cut eight mittens and two hat brims of red construction paper.

Make two eyes per head, following instructions in the front of this book. If you have made some and stored them in a bottle, select four that are alike.

Cut one end of the long green bumps off (about ½″). This piece will go into the bodies (pulp peaks). Tightly curl (bend) the other ends with the long-nosed pliers. Mittens will fit on both sides, glued together. Ice pick holes in opposite sides of each peak body, about halfway up. Put a dot of glue on the end of each chenille bump and insert the arms into these holes.

Paint hair on the other half of the balls. Put a dot of glue on each of the top peaks. Set a head on so the face is not on the side with an arm. Both faces face the same direction. Put a dot of glue on each of the four corners of the body. Stick them on the

artificial grass. Pick them up. Then apply a bigger dot of glue on the artificial grass where the glue spots are. Reset the peaks in the glue.

Trace and cut the hat and mittens from red paper. If you double and staple the paper, two mittens will match when glued back to back over the chenille arm curls.

If the head appears to need more glue around the base, add it with a toothpick. You can pierce three common pins around the head into the peak body to hold the head while it dries. Remove them later.

Put a couple very tiny dots of glue to the face. Transfer eyes with a dampened finger to the face. Make mouth and nostrils with a red marker.

Glue mitten to arms to cover front and back of curled chenille wire. Arms are shaped as illustrated. Glue banner to the inner arms with dots of glue. Glue hat brim in three places and place on heads. Make eyelashes with a black marker. Three to five eyelashes per eye is enough.

# Bird Feeder Ornament

*Materials needed:*
   Clear plastic (two pieces) 2″ x 1½″
   Typing paper (two pieces) 2″ x 1½″
   Corrugated cardboard
   Light cardboard 2⅛″ x 1½″, 2¾″ x 2½″, and
      2″ x 3½″
   Fine vermiculite (for plants)
   Manila construction paper
   Airplane enamel in green, red, and black
   Toothpicks
   6″ green string
   Woodtone wallpaper (optional)
   ¼″ diameter bead
   Hot melt glue in tuna can
   White glue
   #3 double pointed knitting needle
   Ice pick
   Single edge razor blade
   Fingernail scissors (cutting wings and tail)
   Scissors
   Brush (small)
   Electric saber saw with knife-edge blade

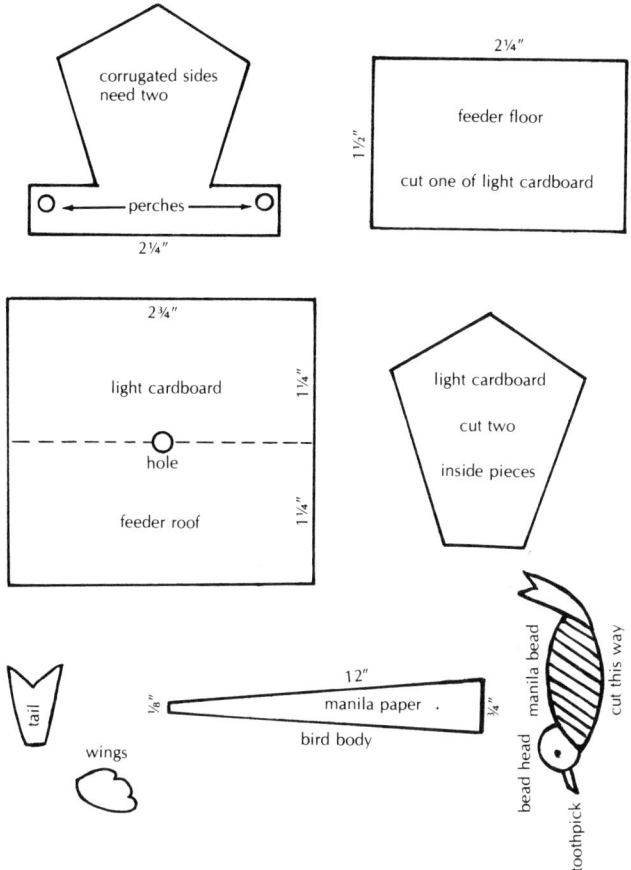

corrugated sides
need two

perches

2¼"

2¼"

feeder floor

cut one of light cardboard

1½"

2¾"

light cardboard

1¼"

hole

feeder roof

1¼"

light cardboard

cut two

inside pieces

tail

12"

wings

⅛"

manila paper ·

bird body

¾"

bead head    manila bead

cut this way

toothpick

*Assembly:*

Cut all parts from materials indicated on patterns. (This ornament may be covered with wood-tone wallpaper if you'd rather not paint it.)

Glue the light cardboard sides to the corrugated (printed side if it has printing) sidepieces, leaving 1/16" along both sides. The clear plastic will fit between these sides. Paint the outside and where the perches will be glued green. Do not paint the light cardboard or perches.

Wind the typing paper (or any similar paper)

pieces on the knitting needle tightly and evenly. With a thin coating of glue, seal the edges. These are the perches.

Score the roof as indicated. If you are covering it with wallpaper, cover it before scoring with a razor blade. Paint the roof red only on top (scored side). Leave it white if white-faced cardboard is used.

Form the manila paper around a knitting needle, starting at the large end. Tightly and evenly wind to the narrow end, sealing it with glue. This is the bird's body. Cut the body as diagramed for the head and tail attachments.

Heat hot melt glue and touch the manila bead end (head) into it. Put the bead onto the manila bead. Touch the toothpick and glue to the head and attach the toothpick beak to the head. Use a twisting movement in working with hot glue because it strings. Attach the wings the same way. If you want two birds (one for the roof), make them both at the same time. (Roof one can be in a flight position, wings upwards and bent slightly outwards after the glue has cooled.) Paint the birds red (or color of choice). Dot the eyes with black enamel.

When all paint is dry, glue the floor under the two corrugated ends, leaving ⅜" at each side. Glue perches between the end pieces as indicated.

With a brush, spread white glue on the inside floor and on both of the light cardboard sides. Press fine vermiculite into the glue. Shake off excess. With the aid of a toothpick, spread glue along the edges of the light cardboard sides. Set the clear plastic on both sides. The clear plastic sets against the floor of the feeder.

Tie a knot close to the gathered ends of the green string, making a loop. Pierce the center of the roof on the scored line. Put on a large dot of white glue. Push the knot of the string through it. Glue the top of the feeder and set it on the roof evenly. Put the birds on with hot glue.

# ANIMAL CRAFTS

## Mr. and Mrs. Rabbit

*Materials needed:*

Two large plastic colored eggs
One cup from white plastic egg carton
(cut around ⅞" from crown to base)
1¼" diameter cardboard tube (make pattern
allowances if needed to be larger)
Three dried star flowers for lady's hat
One larger dried flower and two star flowers for
lady's corsage
One feather (will make several men's hat decorations)
Construction paper to closely match eggs' colors
(ears, lady's hat trim, and lady's base covering)
White construction paper (lady's hat brim, inner
ears, man's hat band)
Black construction paper (man's base covering,
man's hat and bow tie)
Scissors
Fingernail scissors
Ruler
Black and red marker pens
Single edge razor blade
Soft lead pencil (to mark bow tie)
Thick white cement
White glue
Hot melt glue
Tuna can
Toothpick
White felt for man's collar
Colored felt for lady's collar

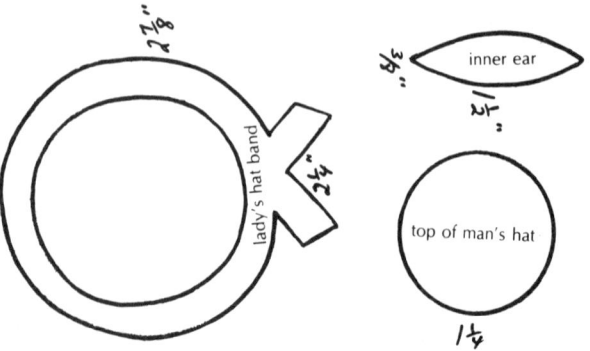

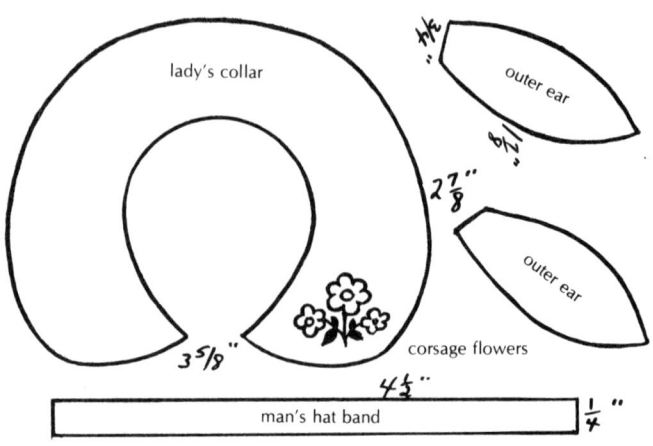

Make a sleeve pattern 1" wide x 5¼" long. Overlap
1" and glue or staple it to form pattern sleeve for
tube tracing.

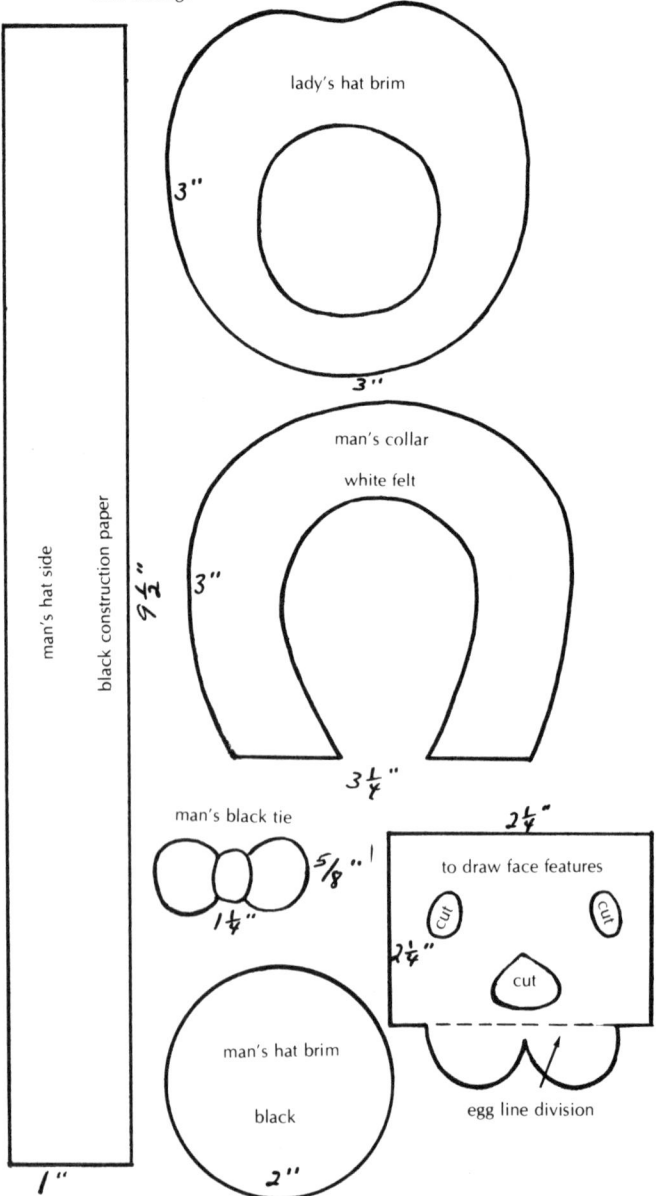

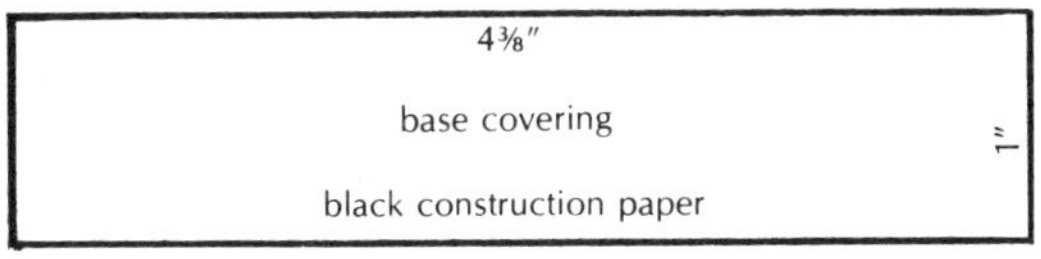

```
┌─────────────────────────────────────────────┐
│                    4⅜"                        │
│                                               │
│              base covering                 1" │
│                                               │
│            black construction paper           │
└─────────────────────────────────────────────┘
```

## Assembly:

Once you cut a cup from the egg carton (longer than the ⅞"), you can trace around it and use it as a pattern, if you are making several rabbit pairs for table decorations, etc. Use the razor blade to cut the egg carton hat crown. Cut all traced parts from paper or felt, as marked. The egg carton crown is attached to the white construction brim with cement or white glue. The brim is glued to the side of the crown. Carefully bring the brim down until it is on the lowest side of the crown. Let dry.

Cut the bases from the tube by sliding the pattern sleeve over the tube. Let the tube rest on the table while you trace around it, to keep it from sliding during the tracing. If you hold it in your hand, it will slip. Eventually you'll have crooked bases that won't stand. Use thick white cement to hold these bases onto the plastic egg heads. The eggs should be tilted back slightly so facial features will be seen easily.

For the man's hat, wind the side (black construction paper strip) around a round glue bottle (1½" diameter). Glue the end to form the round side of the man's hat. Put white glue around the edge of this piece and set it in the center of the larger black circle (brim). Run white glue around the top of the hat (lightly) and set the top (smallest black circle) onto the glued side. After it's completely dry, you can trim away excess construction paper.

The outer ears are the colored ones that should closely match the egg colors, as does the lady's hat ribbon. Fingernail scissors cut circular cuts best. Glue the white inner ears to the colored ear parts, keeping the points even with the ear bases. (Be sure you have two *opposite* ears.)

Cut a feather lengthwise, along the long spine. Discard the fluff you cut off. Cut only through the spine of the feather, at ⅛" intervals. One feather will make approximately one dozen tiny feathers for hats. The seam of the man's hat is in the back. With a dot of white glue, place the tiny feather on the right side of the man's hat. When you put the white band around, make sure it doesn't cover the feather too much. If the feather piece is long, it can be put on touching the base of the side of the man's hat. Start at the back seam with white glue (about two dots) and at each end and wind the band around the man's hat. Glue the construction paper ribbon on the lady's hat. Put three dots of glue or white cement close together on the front of the lady's hat ribbon, just above the brim. Set three star flowers in the glue dots.

Use the facial pattern (of paper, so it'll bend) and trace the mouth and nose with a pencil. You'll add curved lines from the two half circles to form the mouth. With a red marker, first color in the mouth area. With the black marker, carefully trace the penciled lines. Also, fill in the nose area and make three curved eyelashes on each eye.

Cover the bases with black (man) and colored (lady) construction paper, keeping the seam to the back. Try the collars on the bases to fit properly and trim as needed. The lady's should overlap only ⅛", and the man's should have ⅛" gap. Put two dots of glue at the front, one at the center back (close to the top of the base), and wrap the collars around, starting at the front and keeping it close to the top of the bases. Put a dot of glue in the center of the man's collar (at gap) and set the bow tie into it. The lady's collar should be glued at the overlap. With a large dot of white thick cement, place the larger dried flower at the top (with a ¼" stem down) and into the cement. Set two smaller star flowers (no stems) into the cement, hiding the stem of the larger flower. Use a flair pen or a beginner's pencil to curve the lady's hat brim downward. Put white cement here and there, close to the brim and on the inside of the lady's hat, and set the hat on the lady's head.

With fingernail scissors, trim the man's hat. Carefully cut the inside of the brim piece, close to the side of his hat all the way around. (This gives a hole in the hat, so it'll fit on his head.) Put dots of white cement on the inside of his hat, as you did the lady's, and set his hat at a slight angle on his head, to your right as you look at him.

When the hats are dry, heat the hot melt glue in the can at a very low heat until it's melted. Be careful that the heat does not get too warm, or the glue will turn brown, making it more visible on the finished product. It should be just soft enough so you can dip the tip of the diagonal cut of the ear into it. Using a twisting motion, remove it and place the ears in place quickly. (Remember, this glue strings. It will pull off the paper without too much trouble, but it won't pull off the plastic egg.) The man's ears should be placed so the one on your right touches the hat brim (tilted to your right, which should appear just above his eye and back about ¼" from the eye). His other ear is placed ¼" back from the eye, so they look straight. The lady's ears are placed on top the hat brim, covering the ribbon. They flair out, which is the reason the ears have diagonal cuts at the base.

You can cut a small circle of corrugated cardboard, just small enough to slip tightly inside the bases. Glue a small stone to the cardboard and glue around the edge. Slip it just within the bottom of the base of each rabbit. Cover this corrugated piece with the same color of construction paper as the base is. The hidden stone will give the rabbits enough weight to keep them from falling too easily.

Since the mouth features are all at the big end of the plastic egg, and the nose and eyes on the pointed end of the egg (divided), you could fill the eggs with candy as a special treat for children or shut-ins. There are any number of things you could hide inside the eggs, which would also add weight to them.

# Playful Kitten

*Materials needed:*
Light white cardboard
½" bell
Paper punch
Crayons

Wide black marker
Yarn of choice color or colors
½" paper fastener

*Assembly:*
Trace and cut all parts from cardboard. Punch holes where indicated. With marker, make leg marks. Tie bell on a yarn string around the kitten's neck, with the knot behind the body. Glue the rectangle piece (at top and bottom) to the back of the body as indicated by the dotted line on the pattern. Slip tail/paw piece through the rectangle in the back. Put the paper fastener through the holes when you get them in line. The child will color all parts before assembling.

Make a pom-pom from yarn by winding yarn several times around a 1" wide piece of cardboard. Slip another piece of yarn through the loops and tie it securely. Leave at least a 3" string at one end. Cut the other end off about ¼" from the pom-pom. Tie the 3" string to the hole in the paw. Fluff the pom-pom after you have cut through all the loops on the cardboard. Trim the pom-pom so it's reasonably round.

When you pump the kitten's tail, the paw bounces the pom-pom. You might discuss with children the good treatment and care they should give their pets. Pets give many hours of pleasure to us. Kittens are one of God's creatures.

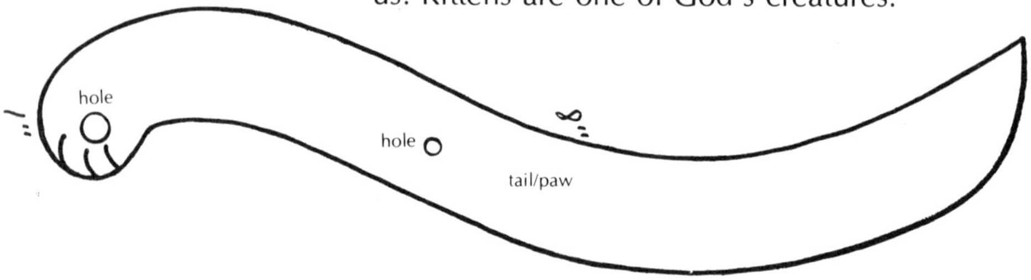

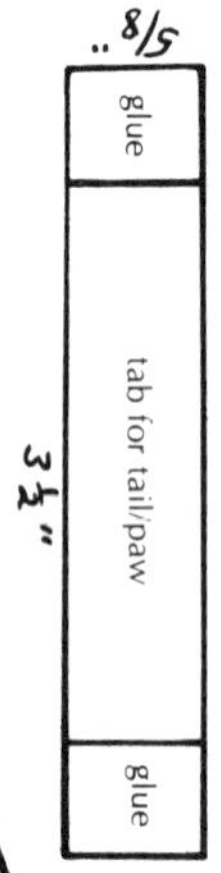

hole

hole

tail/paw

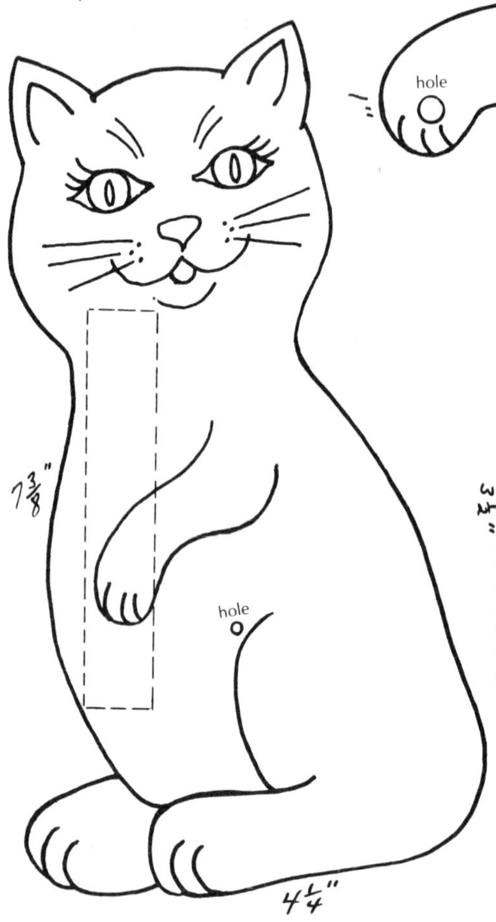

# Seal

5/8"

glue

tab for tail/paw

3½"

glue

7 3/8"

hole

4¼"

*Materials needed:*
4" x 5" piece of white-faced light cardboard
2½" x 3" piece of corrugated cardboard
1" diameter Styrofoam ball
1½" piece of small plastic straw
Crayons

White glue
White and black construction paper
Black marker pen
1½" square of corrugated cardboard
Wallpaper to cover corrugated square
Scissors
Single edge razor blade
⅛" and 3/16" paper punches

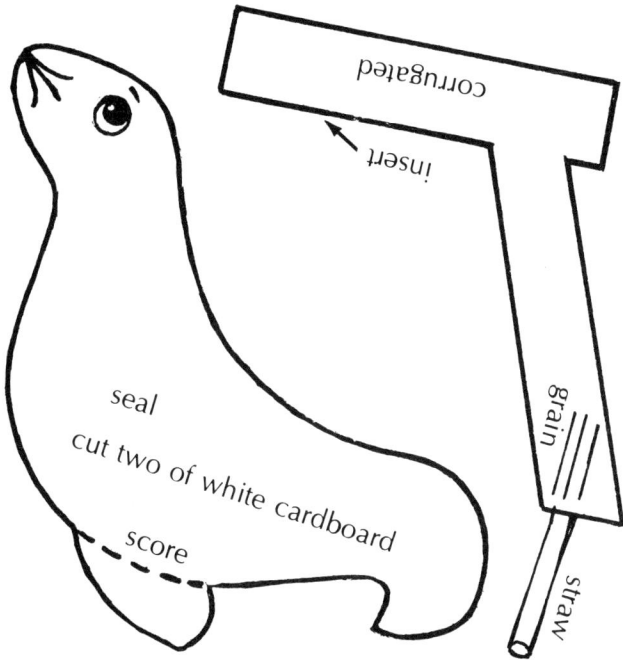

*Assembly:*

Trace and cut out seal. If cardboard is printed on one side, be sure your seals face opposite directions. (Turn pattern over to trace the second seal.) Cut them out and make mouth markings with a black marking pen. Put tiny dots where the eyes will be glued. Color the seal gray. Turn over and lightly score the flipper folding line. Punch black dots from black construction paper with the ⅛" punch. Dip a toothpick in white glue to make very tiny dots of glue on the white construction paper. With a dampened finger, touch the black dot and transfer it to the dot of glue on the white paper. When dry, turn the 3/16" paper punch upside down so you can see through the hole. Punch the dotted white paper so the eye pupil is on the edge of the white circle of the punch hole. With a dot of glue on the marked eyes on the seal, transfer the punched eyes, so the seal is looking at his nose.

Cover the square of corrugated cardboard with wallpaper, including the edges. Edge paper can be cut on a paper cutter. Spread the white glue with a finger to make a neater covered surface. You can spread it thinly.

Cut the inner core from corrugated paper. Be certain you watch the grain of the corrugate care-

fully. The plastic straw must be inserted into a corrugated hole. Glue this piece to the back of one of the seals. Put glue on the opposite side of the corrugated piece and place the other seal on top, being certain they are well aligned. When they are dry, glue the underside of both flippers. Place the seal onto the corrugated square so it's centered. Hold in place with a finger over the flippers. The heat of your finger will help dry the glue. When it will stand alone, allow it to dry by itself.

The Styrofoam ball may be painted with poster paints, spray paints, or colored with crayons. Also, tiny designs from gift wrap may be glued to it. Gouge a straight hole in the ball with fingernail scissors, etc. The hole should be larger than the diameter of the straw, so a child can turn the ball.

Slit the straw up the side about ½" to ¾". Squeeze the slitted end together and insert it into the seal's nose in the corrugated hole. Squeeze a little white glue around the straw. Set the ball on the straw. (It should not quite touch the seal's nose.) Cut a little off the end of the straw to adjust it. If you want the seal to appear to be balancing the straw with a ball on the end of it, make the straw longer in length.

# Lion

*Materials needed:*
White-faced light cardboard 9" x 8"
⅜" paper fastener
Black narrow marking pen
Ice pick
⅛" paper punch
Fingernail scissors (pattern making)
Scissors
3/16" eyes (make them from black and white paper with punches, draw them, or use moveable ones)
Crayons
Single edge razor blade

*Assembly:*
Cut all the parts from cardboard. The face piece is not a part of the patterns in the finished product. (If you cut out and punch out the pieces marked with X, it will enable you to trace many that look

alike.) Use fingernail scissors to cut around tiny places.

Color all parts of the lion after all the lines have been made with a black marker pen. Punch the hole on the lion with the ice pick. Turn over and, in a sawing motion with the razor blade, cut away protruding cardboard. Use the paper punch to make the hole in the legs section. The positioning pattern, which is not part of the finished product, is to be used to mark the back of the lion where the tab will be glued. This is very helpful to a child. Put a fastener through the lion, then through his feet section. Glue both ends of the tab very sparingly with glue. It works best to spread it thinly with your finger. Glue or draw the eyes in place.

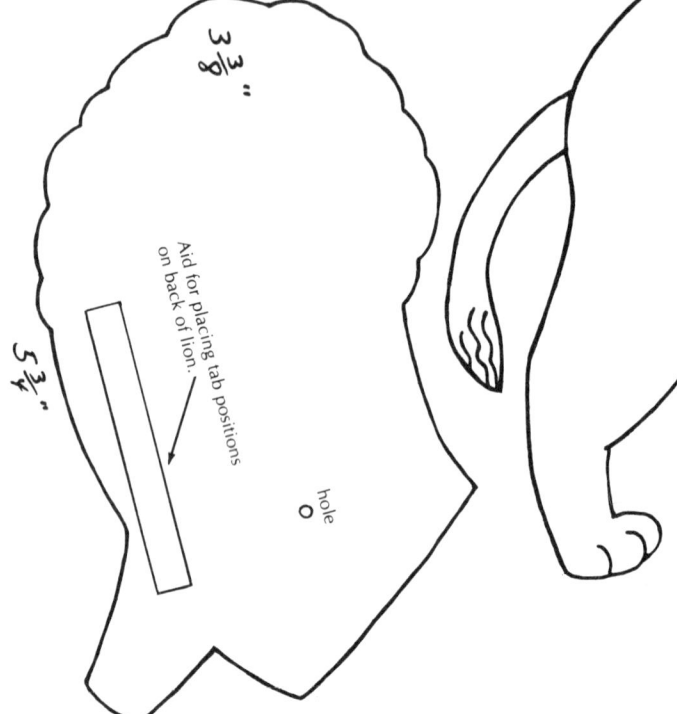

# Kneeling Camel

*Materials needed:*
White-faced light cardboard 8½" x 6"
¼" moving eye (or make your own with paper punches)

Brown or tan construction paper glued over light cardboard (unless you color it)
Two ⅜" paper fasteners
Scissors
⅛" paper punch
Black narrow marking pen
3" x 2¼" colored construction paper (blanket)

*Assembly:*
Trace all pieces onto the construction paper which has been glued to the light cardboard, or on white-faced light cardboard (if the camel is to be colored). Punch holes where indicated. If the camel is to be colored, trace the blanket pattern onto the camel. If the camel is not to be colored, cut the blanket from some bright-colored construction paper. Glue this blanket to the camel's back. Put paper fasteners into the camel and then into his separate leg pieces. The slightly curved leg is the first one on the right. Use the marker to do detailed drawing on the camel. Glue the eye in place.

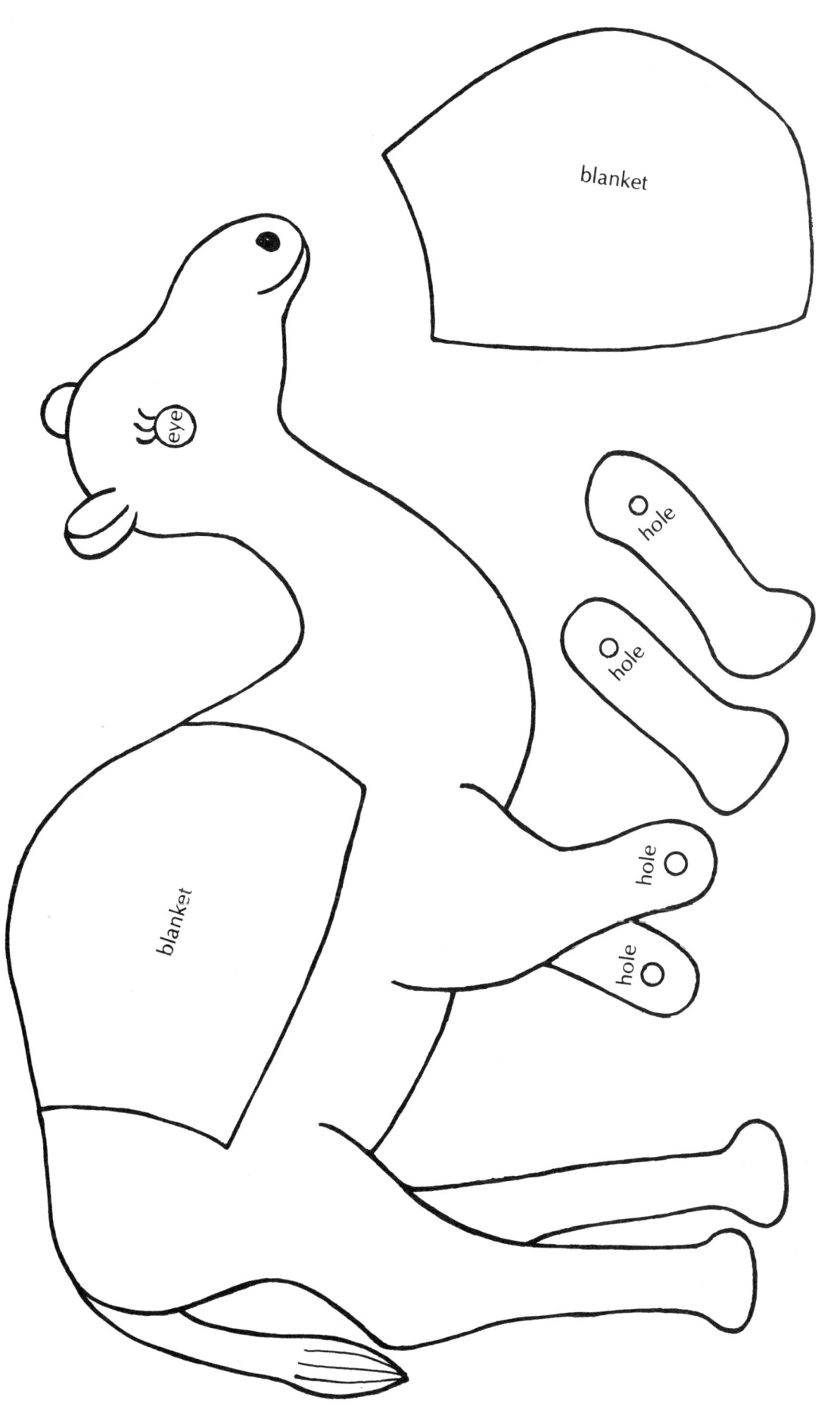

blanket

eye

blanket

hole

hole

hole

hole

# TRAIN CRAFT

right height (1¼" from the bottom). Use a toothpick to put a good sized dot of hot glue where you want the smokestack. It should be toward the front of the train engine (centered). Set the stack into the hot glue. Fill in the gaps around the stack with a tacky glue. When dry, paint the stack, inside and out, with red or whatever is your choice. Retouch anywhere needed with black paint.

## Engine

*Materials needed:*
   Electric saber saw with knife-edge blade
   All corrugated common pattern pieces
   Plastic cup (7 ounce) cut to 1¼" tall
   Hot melt glue in tuna can
   Toothpick
   A tacky glue
   White glue
   Corrugated cardboard 3" x 2¼" (two long sides of cabin)
   Corrugated cardboard 2½" x 2¼" (two short ends of cabin)
   Corrugated cardboard 3½" x 3⅜" (cabin roof)
   Two Jesus seals (#1943 "The Christ" seals—Standard Publishing)
   Two yellow construction paper windows (1¼" x 1½")
   Two yellow construction paper windows (2" x 1¼")
   Acrylic paint in black, wheel color, and red or your choice

*Assembly:*
   Follow directions for "Refrigerator Car," then put top part on. Glue the two 2½" wide ends between the two 3" sides. Glue around the edges of this cabin and center it on the right end. (The open end will be on the front toward you.) Glue around the top edge of the cabin and center the roof on it. If it doesn't seem like it's glued enough, remove it. You can see where the glue lines are. Reglue the roof part and reset it. Glue along all exposed edges and let them dry. Paint the cabin and roof. (Roof can be a different color if desired.) When it is dry, glue the windows in centers of each side. Glue a seal of Jesus to the center of each of the long side windows.
   Melt the hot glue. Cut the plastic cup to the

## Refrigerator Car

*Materials needed:*
   Electric saber saw with knife-edge blade
   Corrugated cardboard for lid, two common ends, two common sides, one common floor
   Typed strip "Refrigerator Car" to glue on front side center
   Acrylic paints for wheel color and another for body color
   Common hinge of white lightweight interfacing
   ¼" paint brush
   White glue

*Assembly:*
   Cut out all parts. (See common parts list.) Glue the two sides to the floor. Glue in both ends. The floor fits between sides and ends. Set the lid on with even overhangs on three sides. The back is flush with the back of the car. Glue half of the hinge to the top of the lid. Then bring the hinge down the back side and glue, spreading the glue with your finger. Glue all exposed edges and let dry. Paint wheels and sides. Paint lid. When dry, glue "Refrigerator Car" strip to center of the side where the lid opens.

## Animal Car

*Materials needed:*
   Electric saber saw with knife-edge blade
   Corrugated pieces (floor, sides, lid, ends) all common patterns
   Black construction paper ¼" wide to go completely around finished car
   Typed strip "Animal Car"
   Wide black marking pen
   Acrylic paint in wheel color and car color
   Ruler
   Pencil

White glue
¼" brush

*Assembly:*

Follow the same assembly as for the "Refrigerator Car." When all paint is dry, glue the strip of black construction paper around the center of the car (all sides), overlapping as needed. *Optional:* Glue a strip at the bottom of the car, if you want a floor. *Also optional:* Glue pictures of animals (small) on two floor levels. Use a ruler and mark off the width of your 12" ruler in diagonal lines (both directions) with a pencil. Go over these penciled lines and the animals with a wide marking pen. Glue the strip, "Animal Car," in the lower righthand corner of the front.

# Caboose

*Materials needed:*

Electric saber saw with knife-edge blade
All corrugated common pattern parts
Corrugated top roof 2½" x 1¾"
Two corrugated cardboard top sides 2" x 1"
Two corrugated cardboard top ends 1" x 1"
Two windows, ½" x 1½" yellow construction paper
Two windows, ½" x ½" yellow construction paper
Acrylic paint in wheel color and red
White glue
Hinge of white lightweight interfacing 1½" x 7"

*Assembly:*

Follow directions for "Refrigerator Car," then put top part on. Glue the two 1" x 1" ends between the 2" long sides. Glue this constructed part to the center of the lid of the caboose. Glue all along the top edges and set the roof part on it. Center the roof so you have an overhang on all sides. Glue exposed edges. Let dry. Paint all the top part. Roof can be a different color if desired. When dry, glue a long window to each long side and a short window to each short end.

# Coal Car

*Materials needed:*

Electric saber saw with knife-edge blade
Corrugated sides (two—see pattern)
Corrugated floor 2¾" x 6¾"
Corrugated ends 2½" x 2¾"
White glue

Two acrylic paint colors (black and wheel color)
¼" brush

*Assembly:*

Cut out all parts. Set ends flush with the outside edges of the sides. Glue floor between the ends and sides. Glue over all exposed edges. Dry. Paint the wheels the same color you use for other train cars. Paint the coal car black.

# Hopper Car

*Materials needed:*

Electric saber saw with knife-edge blade
Corrugated cardboard 7" x 2¾" (ends)
White glue
Three colors of acrylic paint for wheels, hopper, ends
Two rubber bands (to assist in assembly)

*Assembly:*

Cut all parts with the saber saw. To restart sawing in a tight place, put the point of the blade into the uncut area, push down with a firm pressure until the blade is through two thicknesses of the corrugated cardboard. It is best in making these train parts to go through only two thicknesses of cardboard in sawing. This gives more accurate cuts. Follow the traced lines carefully. Keep all printing on the corrugated material to the inside of the car. Lay a wheeled sidepiece on the flat surface. Glue along the bottom floor piece (long side). Lay it just at the top of the wheels, so it is flush with the bottom of the sidepiece.

Glue along two edges of one of the end pieces (fit it first so you will know which two sides to glue). Put it at an angle, 1¼" in from the end of the floor end with the top angled to the top edge of the same sidepiece. Do the other end the same way. Seal all exposed edges with glue, to prepare it for painting. When the glue is dry, paint the wheels the same color as the wheels on the other cars. Paint the hopper, inside and out, with whatever color you select. (See illustration.) Paint the open end and the illusion of open sides a color different from the hopper. This car doesn't have a lid, unless you decide to add one, because hopper cars aren't covered.

# Car Carrier

*Materials needed:*

Electric saber saw with knife-edge blade
White glue

Acrylic paint in two colors, sides and wheels
¼" paint brush
Single edge razor blade
Small amount of white construction paper (cars)
Black narrow marking pen
Hinge 2⅝" x 1¼" (white lightweight interfacing)
Corrugated common floor 6¾" x 2¾"
Corrugated common ends and sides, plus the common floor (top deck—scored)
Two rubber bands

*Assembly:*

Cut all parts with saber saw. Make construction paper tracings of cars. Half the cars will go in opposite directions. Color the cars on opposite sides the same color. Make door and window markings with a black narrow marking pen. If you are using wide marker pens to color the cars, be sure the narrow markings are dry first.

Use the common sidepieces, common ends (one is hinged at the bottom), and two common floor pieces. One common floor piece is scored on top, back 2⅛" from the edge.

Glue the floor between the two sidepieces, as for other cars. Glue the left end piece in place (floor is between all walls). Glue the scored top deck on two long sides and the left short side. The shortest piece from the scored mark is bent downward. It doesn't come to the end of the car. It is about ⅛" back from the hinged door. This deck should be ⅜" down from the top of the car sides. Use a couple rubber bands to hold the sides to the bottom floor and the top deck. Glue half of the hinge to the bottom of the door (right end piece). Glue the other half to the bottom of the floor. Glue all exposed edges and let them dry. When dry, paint the wheels the same color as the other cars. Paint the rest of the carrier another color. When the paint is dry, glue three cars on each side of the lower deck, all facing the glued in end. This gives them the appearance of being on the lower deck.

# Tanker

*Materials needed:*
Electric saber saw with knife-edge blade
Light cardboard (cereal box) 8⅝" plus 1/16" by 6¾" (tank body)
Light cardboard (cereal box) 4½" x 1" (stack)
Silver (foil, etc.) for covering tank and stack, unless painted
Corrugated cardboard floor 7" x 2¾"
Corrugated half wheels (four)
Corrugated ends (two)
Hot melt glue in tuna can

White glue
Rubber cement (unless painting tank)
Ruler
Pencil
Fingernail scissors (to cut tank hole)
Acrylic paint in wheel color, black, and tank color (if painting tank)
Toothpick
¼" brush

*Assembly:*

Cut all pieces of materials listed. Glue half wheels to underneath side of floor, ½" from each end and close to the edge. Dry, then cover all exposed edges with glue. Dry, then paint the wheels the same color you used for other cars of the train. Paint the floor black. It isn't necessary to paint the top of the floor except for about ½" from all edges. Paint the tank body or cover it with foil. (Don't paint or cover the tank body flaps at either end.) If using foil, cover the foil with rubber cement—then the cardboard also. Let it dry. Then stick the two together carefully. The stack is done the same way.

With hot melt glue, glue the stack into a circle. Put a little of the hot glue on half the flat-edge side of the tank end. Run glue along the edge of the rest of the body, but not the other flap. Wind the end around the body. When you come to the flap, again attach it with hot glue. Do the opposite end the same way, squeezing it in. Keep ends flush with the edge of the body. Set the stack in place. Run glue (white) around the outside joint.

Glue a tiny square of light Velcro at each end of the floor, underneath, if desired.

Glue the two flaps of the tank body and set them evenly onto the wheeled floor piece. The tanker would make an ideal bank. The whole train is great for storage of small items such as crayons, pens, jewelry, pins, etc.

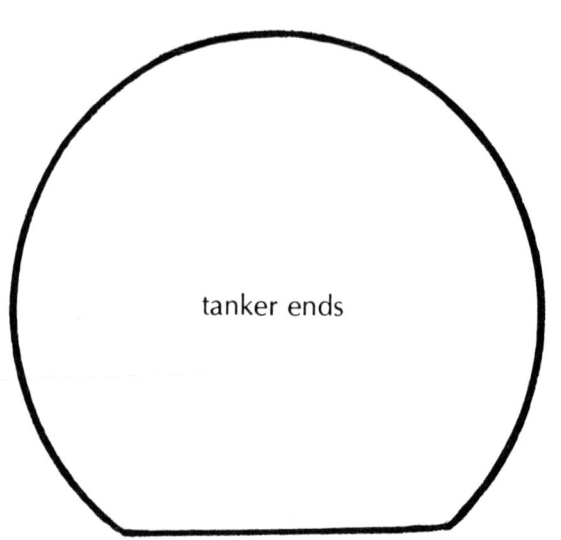

tanker ends

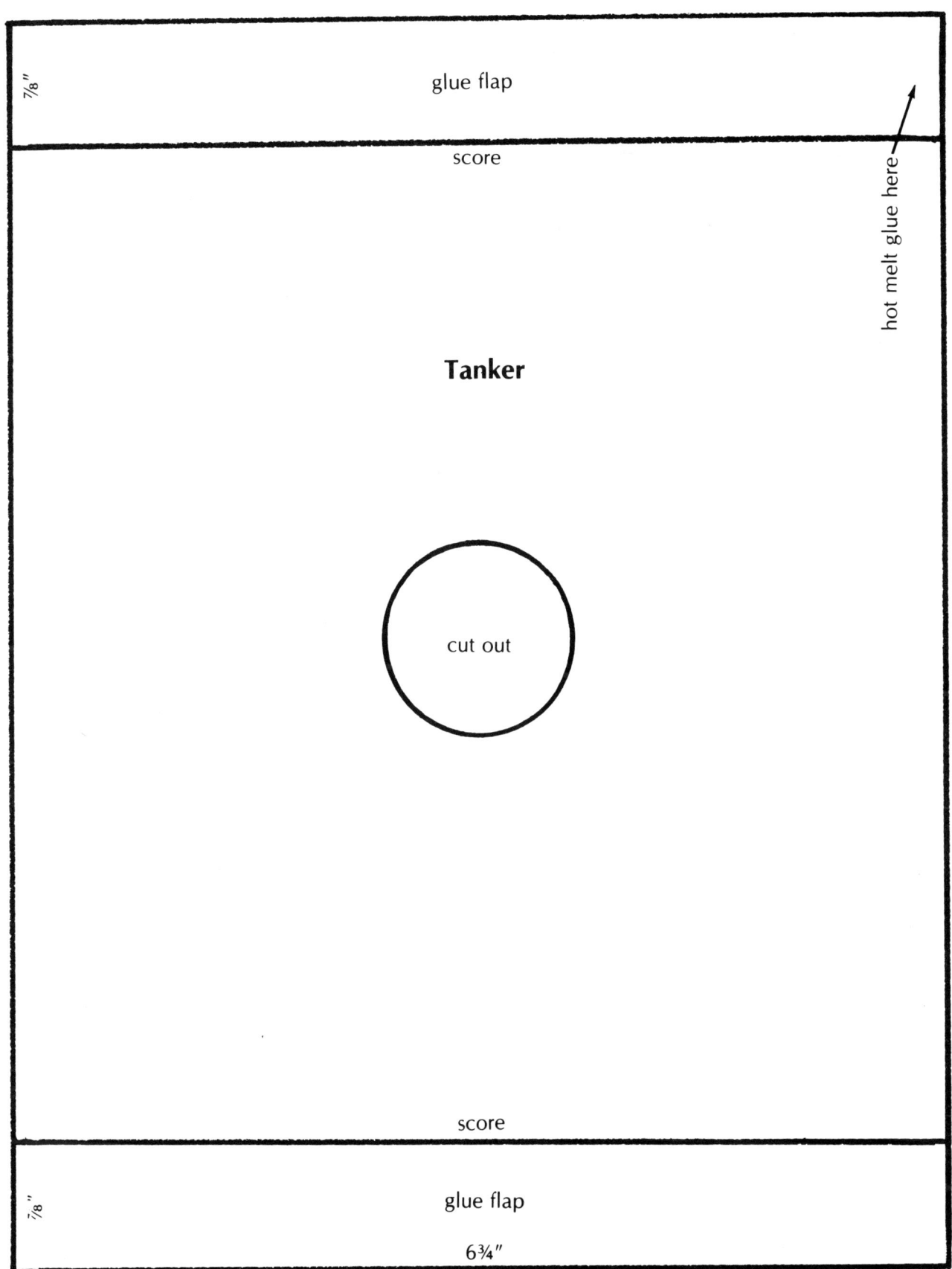

glue flap

⅞"

score

hot melt glue here

**Tanker**

cut out

score

⅞"

glue flap

6¾"

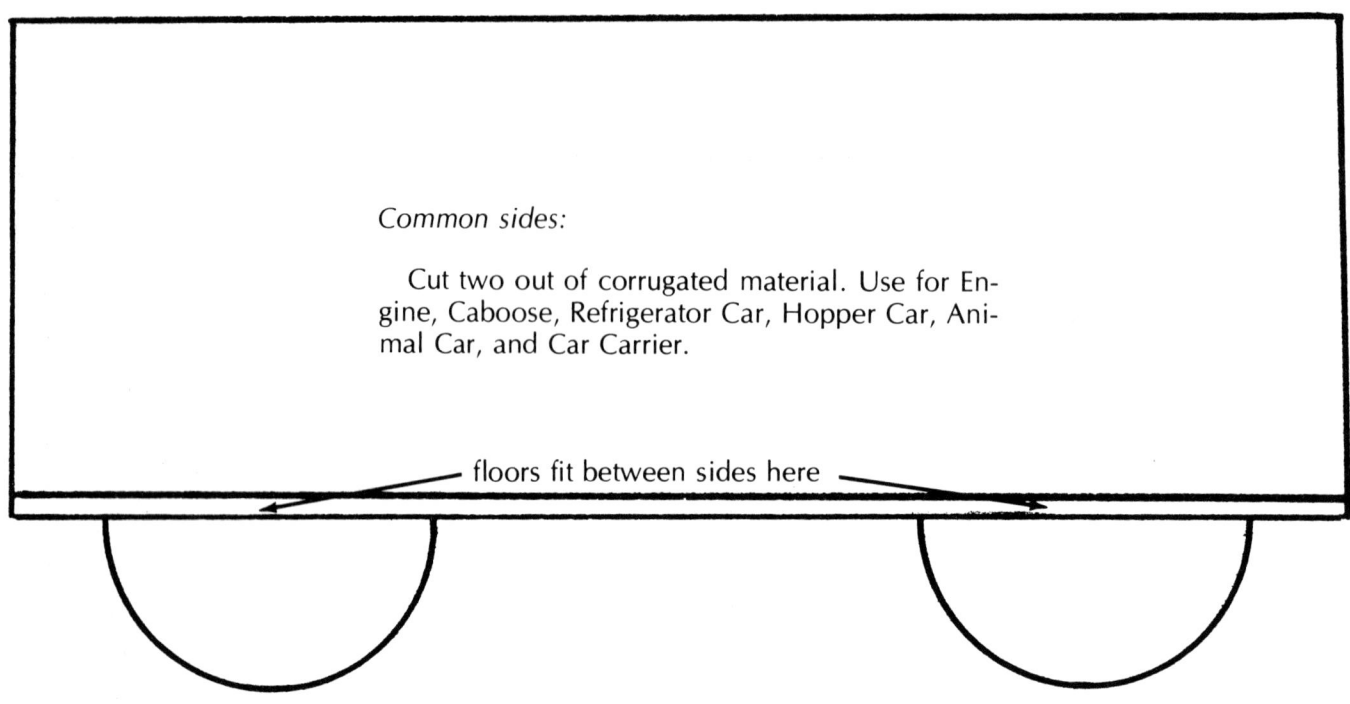

*Common sides:*

Cut two out of corrugated material. Use for Engine, Caboose, Refrigerator Car, Hopper Car, Animal Car, and Car Carrier.

— floors fit between sides here —

*Common patterns:*

Common floor is 6¾″ long and 2¾″ wide
Common ends are 2¾″ wide and 2½″ tall
Common hinge is 7″ x 1½″
Common lid is 7½″ x 3⅜″ (overlapped on 3 sides)

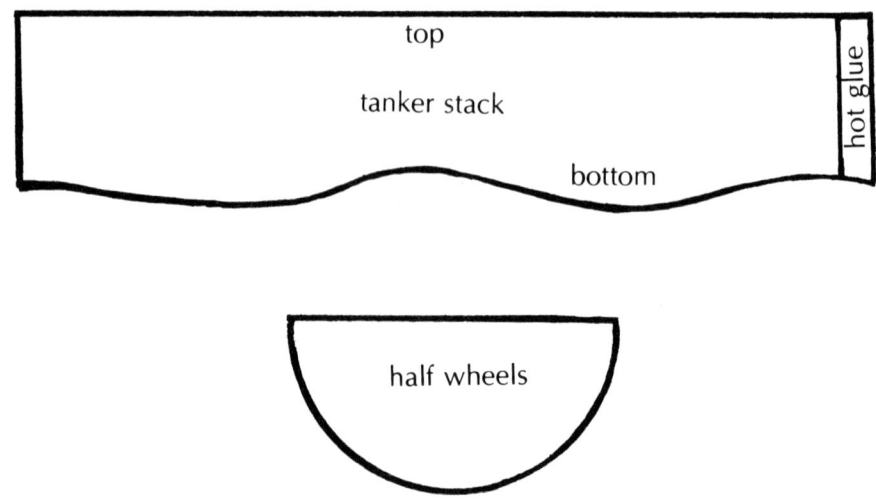

top

hot glue

tanker stack

bottom

half wheels

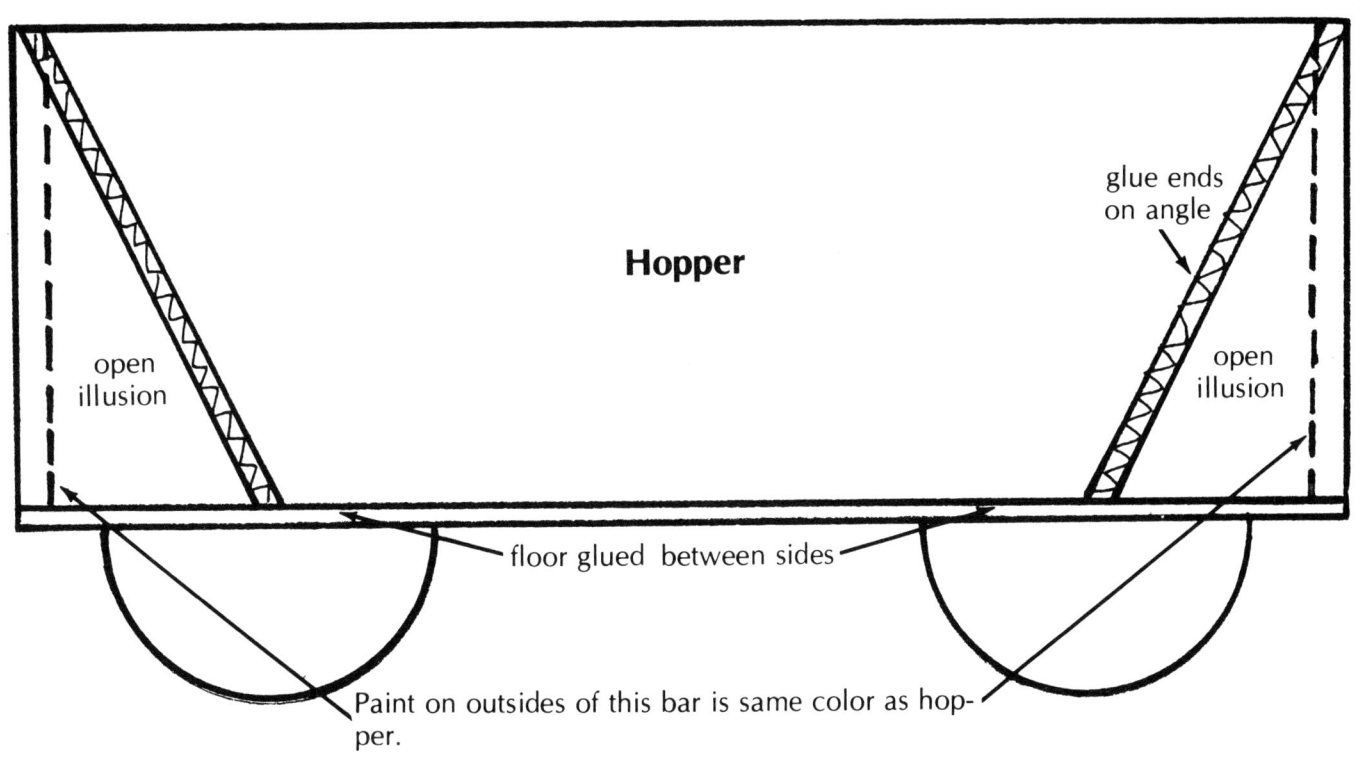

**Hopper**

glue ends
on angle

open
illusion

open
illusion

floor glued between sides

Paint on outsides of this bar is same color as hopper.

**Car Carrier**

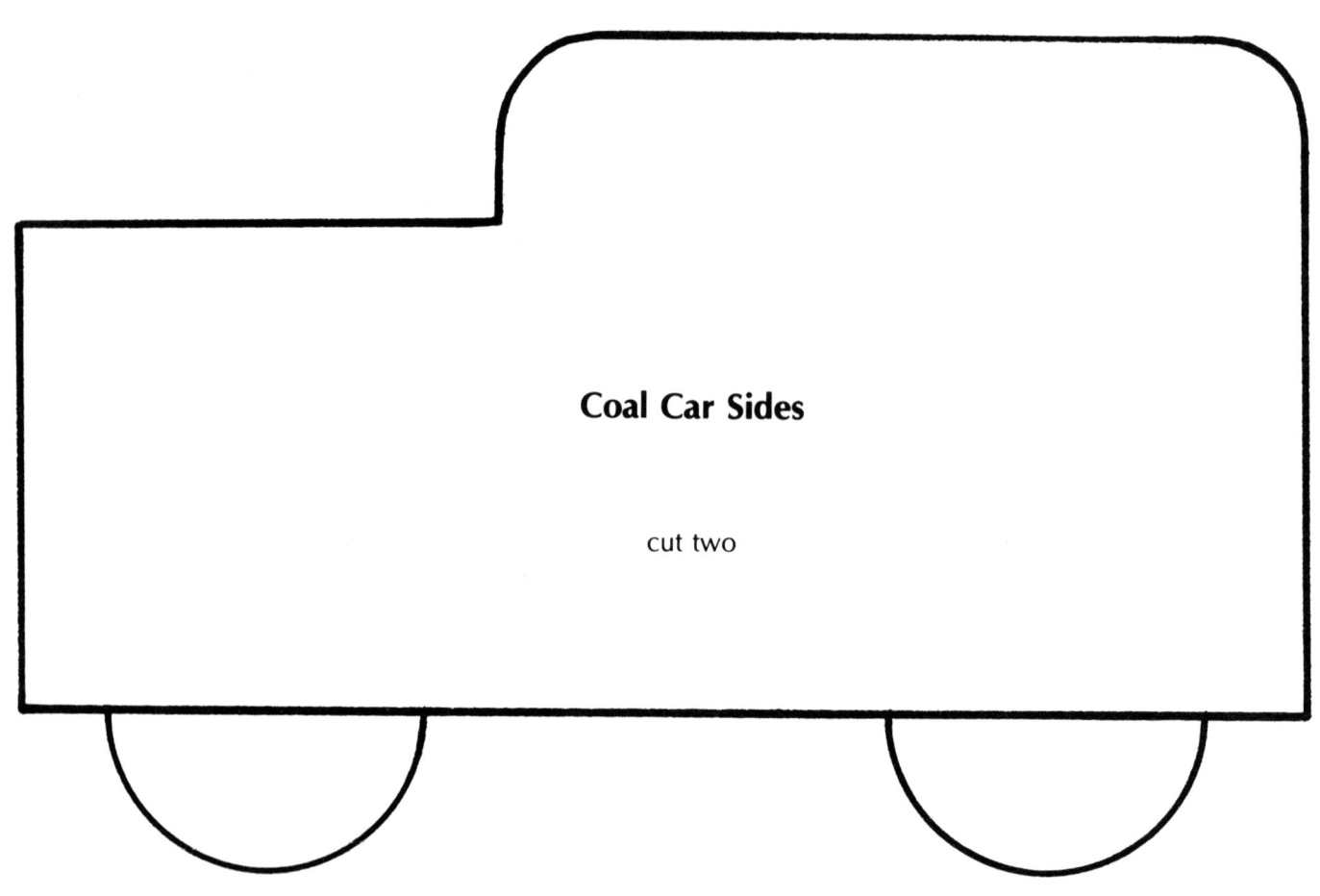

## Coal Car Sides

cut two

*Coupling cars:* If you wish to couple the cars, you can use a small square (½″ x ½″) glued to the under floor of both ends of all cars except the engine and caboose. Glue square to only one end of these cars. A separate strip 1¼″ to 1½″ long can be attached to any two cars to join them.

# OTHER CRAFT BOOKS FOR YOUR LIBRARY